TOWARD A PHILOSOPHICAL THEORY OF EVERYTHING

TOWARD A PHILOSOPHICAL THEORY OF EVERYTHING

Contributions to the Structural-Systematic Philosophy

ALAN WHITE

B L O O M S B U R Y

NEW YORK • LONDON • NEW DELHI • SYDNEY

Bloomsbury Academic

An imprint of Bloomsbury Publishing Inc

1385 Broadway	50 Bedford Square
New York	London
NY 10018	WC1B 3DP
USA	UK

www.bloomsbury.com

Bloomsbury is a registered trade mark of Bloomsbury Publishing Plc

First published 2014

Library of Congress Cataloging-in-Publication Data
White, Alan, 1951-
Toward a philosophical theory of everything : contributions to the structural-systematic philosophy / Alan White. – 1st [edition].
pages cm
Includes bibliographical references.
ISBN 978-1-62356-718-7 (hardback : alk. paper) 1. Philosophy. I. Title.
BD21.W455 2014
149'.97–dc23
2013034732

ISBN: HB: 978-1-6235-6634-0
PB: 978-1-6235-6718-7
ePDF: 978-1-6235-6034-8
ePub: 978-1-6235-6627-2

Typeset by Fakenham Prepress Solutions, Fakenham, Norfolk NR21 8NN
Printed and bound in the United States of America

For my mother, Anne Stelzenmuller White,
and my mother-in-law, Scotty Nicholls

CONTENTS

ACKNOWLEDGMENTS

First and above all, I must thank Lorenz B. Puntel for welcoming me as a collaborating contributor to the structural-systematic research program in philosophy, first while *Structure and Being* and *Being and God* were being written, and now as author of this book. His generosity, clarity, and acumen have decisively influenced my philosophical development, and working with him continues to be a source of immense satisfaction.

My thanks also to Williams College and its Oakley Center for the Humanities and Social Sciences, which provided me with course release to work on the book, and sponsored a faculty seminar devoted to it, during which I had fruitful discussions with my Williams colleagues Will Dudley (Philosophy), Tom Garrity (Math), Tom Kohut (History), and Bernie Rhie (English). More recently, Williams students Emily Stein and Taylor Oddleifson, and Fordham graduate student Rory Misiewicz, commented helpfully on near-final versions of the complete text. Stein's work was funded by Williams College's Class of 1957 Summer Research Program, for whose support I am also grateful. Individual chapters have benefited from discussions with students in various sections of my introductory course "Truth, Goodness, and Beauty."

Finally, my deep thanks to Sandy Thatcher, editor for *Structure and Being* and valued adviser, concerning *Being and God* and this book, following his retirement.

FOREWORD

I was delighted to have the opportunity to write this Foreword for *Toward a Philosophical Theory of Everything* (*TAPTOE*), a book devoted to what it aptly terms the structural-systematic research program in philosophy. I have been working on this program since the late 1970s, and *TAPTOE* author Alan White has been working on it with me since fall 2003. Our collaboration continues with *TAPTOE* in that the two of us have discussed the book in its entirety.

What is most important for me to say in this Foreword is the following: *TAPTOE* succeeds magnificently in accomplishing its two chief goals, that is, in providing a concise and accessible introduction to the structural-systematic research program as a whole, and in making important contributions to the structural-systematic philosophy—the theory to which the research project is devoted. It does the latter particularly in its Chapter 6, which presents a theory of human freedom, and its Chapter 7, which presents a theory of beauty that increases the intelligibility and coherence of the structural-systematic philosophy as presented in *Structure and Being*.

Lorenz B. Puntel
Munich-Augsburg, April 2013

1

Preliminaries

Some readers of this sentence, the first in this book, may have been led to do so because they were attracted by the prospect of learning about work toward a philosophical theory of everything. Others may be motivated instead by incredulity: How could there be a *philosophical* theory of everything—or, perhaps, even of anything? These are good questions, and this book aims to give them good answers, beginning with explanations of the subtitle (1.1) and title (1.2), the latter of which, despite its apparent outrageousness, did not prevent readers of these words from getting to this point.

1.1 An initial clarification of this book's subtitle

For sake of brevity, this book's subtitle speaks of the structural-systematic philosophy (SSP). Clarity is served, however, by speaking as well of the structural-systematic research program in philosophy (SSRPP). This program is undertaken but far from completed in *Structure and Being* (Puntel 2008; *SB*) and *Being and God* (Puntel

2011; *BG*).[1] *SB*, particularly, establishes the SSRPP as a *research program* in philosophy by articulating it in sufficient detail to enable other philosophers—including this book's author and, potentially, any of its readers—to contribute to it. As explained below (Chapter 2), *SB* presents the abstract theoretical framework for the SSP—the theory to which the SSRPP is devoted—but it does not come close to concretizing that framework in complete detail. It thus opens the way for other philosophers—again, including this book's author—to contribute to the SSRPP in three distinct ways. First, others can treat in greater detail subject matters, such as ethics and human freedom, that *SB* treats only relatively briefly. Second, others can investigate subject matters, including for example political philosophy and the ontology of time, that *SB* does not treat at all. Third, because *SB* (475–6, 482–3) both explicitly acknowledges that its presentation of the SSP can be improved, and explains how it can be improved, others can offer such improvements.

This book—*TAPTOE*—aims to contribute to the SSP in the first and third of the ways just identified. It supplements *SB* and *BG* by providing (Chapters 1–2) a clear and concise introduction to the SSRPP and by presenting (Chapters 3–6, Chapter 8) alternative accounts and—particularly in the case of human freedom—more extensive accounts than are to be found in *SB* or *BG*. It aims to improve on the concretization of the SSP presented in *SB* by introducing, as an alternative to *SB*'s (4.4) treatment of the aesthetic world, a sketch (Chapter 7) of a theory of beauty.

---

[1] Neither *SB* nor *BG* uses the phrase "research program in philosophy"; in introducing it, this book makes explicit a thesis implicit in the two other books.

That *SB*'s presentation of the SSP can be improved on and expanded reveals, to be sure, *SB*'s self-acknowledged imperfection and incompleteness, but—far more importantly—it also reveals the viability and strength of the structural-systematic research program in philosophy to which *SB* is devoted.

1.2 An initial clarification of this book's title

For two central reasons, the project indicated by the title of this book—*Toward a Philosophical Theory of Everything*—can easily appear, early in the twenty-first century, to be, at best, quixotic. The first reason is that the term "theory of everything" is commonly associated not with philosophy but with physics. The second reason is that even those who consider philosophy to be a discipline that produces theories (of whatever quality) appear virtually universally to deny that it should or even could undertake the task of producing a theory that is, in any reasonable and defensible sense, *of everything*. The purpose of this section is to show that neither of these reasons is a good one for rejecting the project of developing just such a theory.

This section treats first the question of the subject matter (or matters) that do or should qualify as philosophical, because treating that question contributes to clarifying how philosophical theories of everything differ from theories situated in contemporary physics. The section relies on various terms and distinctions that are sufficiently clear for its purposes but whose adequate explanations are provided only in later sections.

"Philosophy" is a word whose history spans nearly two and a half millennia. Within that period, the word has been used in various different and often contradictory ways, so it is not surprising that it (and with it "philosophical," etc.) has come to have various distinct meanings both in ordinary and in academic English (and in other languages in which cognates of it appear). As is hinted at above and clarified below, in this book "philosophy" designates a strictly *theoretical* endeavor—not one that (for example) aims to change anyone's life or make anyone happy (although of course some books called "philosophical" do aim to do those things, and although this book will have effects on its readers' lives).

In the time of Aristotle (the fourth century BCE)—relatively shortly after the coinage of the term *"philosophia"* in ancient Greece—all theoretical inquiry could be classified as *philosophical* inquiry.[2] For this reason, there were at that time no restrictions on the subject matter potentially available to philosophical theorization. In a technical term clarified below, the universe of philosophical discourse was unrestricted. This largely continued to be the case until around the seventeenth century, when what came to be classified as non-philosophical modes of theorization—non-philosophical sciences—began to develop; their development required *restricting* their universes of discourse. Of central importance to the project undertaken in this book is the question of what then happens to philosophy. In his *Philosophy 1: A Guide Through the Subject*, A. C. Grayling (1999: 2) answers that question as follows:

---

[2] This broad sense of "philosophy" is retained in, for example, sections 1 and 4(a) in the section on the word in the *Oxford English Dictionary* (*OED*). As the *OED*'s section 1 notes, this broad sense explains why academic doctorates are doctorates *of philosophy* (PhDs).

one can see philosophy as having given birth in the seventeenth century to natural science, in the eighteenth century to psychology, and in the nineteenth to sociology and linguistics; while in the twentieth century it has played a large part in the development of computer science, cognitive science, and research into artificial intelligence. No doubt this oversimplifies the role of philosophical reflection, but it does not much exaggerate it, because in effect philosophy consists in inquiry into anything not yet well enough understood to constitute a self-standing branch of knowledge. When the right questions and the right methods for answering them have been identified, the field of inquiry in question becomes an independent pursuit.

Grayling is not alone. Indeed, the prominent analytic metaphysician Peter van Inwagen goes so far as to say (2008b: 11), of the view expressed by Grayling, that "most people who have thought about the matter would take this"—that is, the restriction of philosophy to subject matters that are not (yet) claimed by sciences—"to be one of the defining characteristics of philosophy."

In considering the position taken by Grayling and van Inwagen, it is important to ask the following question: according to what theory or theoretician is philosophical inquiry not scientific? Or, more specifically, within the theorization of what universe of discourse could the sentence "Philosophical inquiry is not scientific" emerge? Unquestionably, that sentence, as it is (implicitly) understood by Grayling and van Inwagen, cannot emerge within any theory having a restricted universe of discourse. Why not? Precisely because its articulation presupposes that *the unrestricted universe of discourse is* divided into *restricted universes of discourse* of two kinds, and that those are the only kinds of universes of discourse that there are: there are the restricted ones that are well-enough understood to be studied by distinct sciences, and there are the restricted ones that are not, and are therefore (for now) left to philosophy.

What does this show? Three things. First, that if every theoretical discipline must have a *restricted* universe of discourse, then *no* discipline can develop theories about *the unrestricted universe of discourse*. Second, that one cannot present a theory about how all the restricted universes of discourse of the various restricted inquiries relate to one another and to philosophy's universe (or perhaps universes) of discourse *unless* one thematizes the unrestricted universe of discourse (and that is precisely what both Graying and van Inwagen do, albeit—again—only implicitly). Third, that if the subject matter for philosophy is indeed that which has not been claimed by any non-philosophical science then, *if the unrestricted universe of discourse is or can or must be a subject matter for theoretical inquiry,* it is a subject matter that non-philosophical sciences, which are individuated by their restricted universes of discourse, *must* leave to philosophy.

As may be evident from the preceding paragraph, the task of developing a philosophical theory of everything begins to come into view if the development of the non-philosophical sciences is taken not to *restrict* philosophy's universe of discourse but instead to *clarify* a universe of discourse that *can* be a subject matter *only* for philosophy. Prior to modernity, because philosophy could thematize *anything*—including any *restricted* universe of discourse—it was often far from obvious that philosophy could or should thematize *everything,* understanding "everything" to mean the *unrestricted* universe of discourse. In the so-called analytic philosophy predominant at present in much of the world, the situation is yet worse, because analytic philosophers tend to adopt the divide-and-conquer strategy that has served particularly the natural sciences so well: they work in the currently recognized areas of specialization in philosophy—ethics, metaphysics, philosophy of language, philosophy of mind, and so forth—making few if any attempts to determine how all these areas might fit together.[3] As a consequence, the SSP's subject matter—the unrestricted universe of discourse—cannot come into their view.[4]

Because the unrestricted universe of discourse includes everything (in at least some significant sense of "everything"), a philosophical theory whose subject matter is the unrestricted universe of discourse

---

[3] Soames 2003, *Philosophical Analysis in the Twentieth Century*, describes the analytic philosophy of the thirty years preceding its publication as follows (463):

> Philosophy has become a highly organized discipline, done by specialists primarily for other specialists. The number of philosophers has exploded, the volume of publications has swelled, and the subfields of serious philosophical investigation have multiplied. Not only is the broad field of philosophy today far too vast to be embraced by one mind, something similar is true even of many highly specialized subfields.

Nine years later, Schwartz 2012, *A Brief History of Analytic Philosophy: From Russell to Rawls*, (299–300) comments:

> The only qualm I have about Soames' statement is his claim that "philosophy has become a highly organized discipline." I'm not sure what he means by that, but "highly *dis*organized discipline" would seem like a truer description given the rest of what he says.

[4] "Continental philosophy," throughout the twentieth century the most significant alternative to analytic philosophy, suffers less from problems of fragmentation than from ones of intelligibility. *BG*'s Chapter 2 exposes many such problems in the works of Martin Heidegger, and its Chapter 4, many in the works of Emmanuel Levinas and Jean-Luc Marion.

is a philosophical theory of everything. To leave open the possibility that philosophical theories may have restricted universes of discourse (as, currently, most do), the SSRPP designates the philosophy whose subject matter is the unrestricted universe of discourse *systematic philosophy.*

Given the preceding account, it is easy to explain—indeed, it may well already be obvious—why no theory presented by contemporary physics could be a "theory of everything" of the sort that a philosophical theory of everything would be: contemporary physics has as its subject matter a *restricted* universe of discourse. This point is clearly articulated by the prominent mathematical physicist Roger Penrose (t' Hooft et al. 2005: 259):

> The terminology 'theory of everything' has always worried me. There is a certain physicist's arrogance about it that suggests that knowing all the physical laws would tell us everything about the world, at least in principle. Does a physical theory of 'everything' include a theory of consciousness? Does it include a theory of morality, or of human behaviour, or of aesthetics? Even if our idea of science could be expanded to incorporate these things, would we still think of it as 'physics,' or would it even be reducible to physics?

"Our idea of science" is considered just below, but even without such consideration it is fully clear that physics as it is *now* cannot develop theories about all the subject matters Penrose lists. The *philosophical* theory of everything to which this book aims to contribute, on the other hand, must include theories of consciousness, of morality, of some aspects of human behaviour, and of aesthetics—as well as, in a sense and a manner explained below, everything else. It is important to emphasize at the outset, however, that although this philosophical theory of everything is *holistic* in the sense of being comprehensive, it is not *imperialistic* in that it in no way aims to *replace* any of the non-philosophical sciences.

As for "our idea of science": as suggested by the clarification above of what the word "philosophy" means in this book—and as explained in greater detail below (2.5)—ordinary language does not determine how the SSP uses words that it draws from that language.[5] According to the SSP, theoretical inquiry within any current academic discipline can be scientific. Whether any specific such inquiry qualifies as scientific is determined not by the inquiry's subject matter, but instead—again relying on a term clarified below—by the quality of the theoretical framework that inquiry relies on. The SSP, relying as it does on a clearly articulated theoretical framework, classifies itself as a science, and indeed, because of the comprehensiveness of its subject matter, as the universal science (see *SB* 10, 17, 356, 477f, 481ff).

One additional aspect of the Grayling passage quoted above can now be fruitfully considered. Each science—each non-philosophical science, in the terminology of the SSP—is, according to Grayling, "a self-standing branch of knowledge," an "independent pursuit." What might be meant here by "self-standing" or "independent," and what by "knowledge"? Presumably, a science is a branch of *knowledge* only if, one way or another, it presents linguistic accounts—theories— that are true, in some sense of "true." But how is it that there can be linguistic accounts that are true—how is it that languages can

---

[5] As indicated above (1.1), the SSP is the theory to which the SSRPP is devoted.

articulate the subject matters of the relevant theories? And what is the appropriate sense of "true"? The non-philosophical sciences presuppose—generally implicitly—one or another answer to each of these questions (and to many more), but cannot raise these questions, precisely because the questions cannot be raised within the restricted universes of discourse of those sciences. As a consequence, those sciences are *not* self-standing or independent at least in that they "stand" or depend on what they presuppose but cannot investigate. What they presuppose but cannot investigate can and must, however, be investigated by systematic philosophy.

An additional point important to this section begins by noting that there is a phrase at least roughly synonymous with "theory of every-thing," as that phrase is used to name a theory within the science of physics. The second phrase is "final theory," as used, for example, in Steven Weinberg's *Dreams of a Final Theory* (Weinberg 1992). The SSP, if completed, would be a philosophical theory of everything, but would not in any way be a *final* theory. As explained more fully below and in various places in *SB*, the SSP aims to be *the best currently available* systematic philosophy, hence the best currently available philosophical theory of everything. If it succeeds in being the best currently available systematic philosophy, then it is—by its own self-assessment—better than is any available alternative, but it is *not* closer to some hypothesized *final* systematic philosophy, because it denies the intelligibility of the notion of a final systematic philosophy (see 2.3). In addition, even if it is the best currently available systematic philosophy, the SSP *explicitly acknowledges* that it may someday be supplanted by a superior theory, and it indicates how that supplanting would be accomplished (see *SB*, 644–6).

1.3 Preliminary remarks on methodology

The philosophical theory of everything of which this book is a partial presentation is a linguistic account that is true. At this point, "true" can be understood in the everyday sense in which, roughly, a given sentence is true if it says that such-and-such is the case, and such-and-such is indeed, or in actuality, the case (the sense of "true" specific to the SSP is explained below; see 2.5 and Chapter 3). The development and to some extent the presentation of this theory are guided by a method that is further clarified in 2.2, 2.5, and 2.6 (and *SB* 1.4), but some preliminary methodological remarks are appropriate at this point. The chief reason for this is that *TAPTOE* aims at maximal clarity, and that includes clarity concerning the status of its own sentences.

To be clarified at this point, in a general manner, are the criteria that the sentences presented in this account must satisfy if they are to qualify as true. Negatively, the account's method does *not* require—and indeed does not allow—for it to begin with or to include any sentences that qualify as *foundational* by satisfying both of the following two conditions: (a) being self-evidently or indubitably or in some way non-problematically true, and (b) providing premises from which all true sentences *not* satisfying condition (a) would have to be derived. Positively, the method requires instead, from the outset, (1) that its sentences be adequately intelligible (loosely, that they not be nonsensical or meaningless), (2) that they not be defective in ways that would preclude the possibility of their being true (thus, most clearly, that they not be self-contradictory), and (3) that they be mutually consistent (that they not contradict one another). As additional sentences are added, the method comes to require that, in addition to satisfying the three criteria just identified, these sentences also serve in some cases to increase the intelligibility of previously introduced sentences or groups of sentences (arguments, subtheories, and so forth) and, in all cases, ultimately to increase the intelligibility, coherence, and comprehensiveness, with respect to its subject matter, of the account as a whole.

Differently put, this account is structured as a holistic network of sentences collectively constituting a partial presentation of a philosophical theory of everything or (technically) of being. Nodes within the network—individual theses and later subtheories—are stabilized by means of inferential interlinkings of various sorts, including deduction, induction, and—especially—inferences to the best explanation, theorization, or systematization (see *SB* 1.4.2). Obviously, the sentences in this account must be presented sequentially; for this reason, sentences articulated as the account begins cannot, when initially presented, be tightly inferentially linked to many (if any) other sentences. To the extent that the account is successful, linkages both multiply and strengthen as the account proceeds. Thus, for example, the intelligibility and coherence (within the book as a whole) of this section's description of its method should increase as the density of the presented network increases, as should that of the SSP's reliance on the network-structure.

The increasing density of the network is also accompanied by increasing refinement. The reason for this is that clarity and intelligibility are often served by, and in many cases indeed require, initial reliance on formulations that prove, in light of subsequently introduced terms, theses, and arguments, to be less than fully adequate.

Thus, for example, when such technical terms as "philosophical theory of everything," "unrestricted universe of discourse," and "being as such and as a whole" are initially introduced they are of necessity relatively vague; their vagueness decreases as the account develops. This holds as well, of course, for the terms "intelligibility" and "coherence"; the terms are drawn from ordinary English, and the meanings of these terms that are specific to the SSP are made increasingly clear as the account progresses.

To put the central point of the two preceding paragraphs more directly and colloquially: the reader should be guided implicitly, upon encountering a given sentence or group of sentences in this book, not (in the overwhelming majority of cases) by such questions as "Is this true?", "Has this been proved?", or "Do I agree?", but instead by the questions (i) "Does this make sense?",[6] (ii) "*Is it possible* that this is true?", and (iii) "How does this fit together with what has come before?". As the account develops, it becomes increasingly appropriate for the reader to keep in mind the additional question, (iv) "In what ways and to what degrees does this sentence or group of

---

[6] The relevant question is *not* the *pragmatic* (subject- or reader-related) question, "Does this make sense *to me*?", but instead the *semantic* (language- or meaning-related) question, "Does this make sense *in the language in which it is expressed*?". To clarify: the sequence "is or tomato anxiously," presented simply as such, makes no sense *in ordinary English* (although it could make sense in some other language, for example in a code, or even in ordinary English if presented *not* simply as such, but instead, say, as a response to the instruction, "Produce a list consisting of a verb, a conjunction, a noun, and an adverb"). In contrast, the sentence "The structural-systematic philosophy is a theory of being as such and as a whole" might well at least initially make relatively little sense *to many readers* who are quite competent in English, but it cannot be identified as *nonsensical* in English. Its attaining adequate *semantic* intelligibility *within this book* requires the introduction of other sentences explaining it and linking it to other sentences, and its adequate *pragmatic* intelligibility—its making adequate sense *to readers*—depends in part, of course, on the readers' own efforts.

sentences increase the intelligibility and coherence of the theory or theories within which it is situated?". Ultimately, assuming that as it develops it adequately satisfies the criteria identified in questions (i)–(iv), the SSP as a whole must be assessed for its theoretical adequacy and indeed for its truth—but because of its network-structure, it can be assessed *only* ultimately, and *not*, as is the case with foundationally structured theories (see 2.2, below), starting from the beginning and continuing with every additional step. Just how the theory is best assessed is a question addressed by the theory itself; how this is accomplished, and why its accomplishment involves no problematic circularity, is explained in detail in *SB* (1.5.2.2–1.5.2.3, 6.3.2.1).

1.4 A philosophically consequent stylistic peculiarity

A stylistic feature that *TAPTOE* shares with *SB* and (generally) *BG*, and one that is unusual in philosophical (and other) literature, is that it speaks of itself rather than of its author. Particularly *TAPTOE* and *SB* rely minimally (if at all) on formulations like "I hold that" or "As the author notes in Chapter 1." There are two basic reasons for this. The first is that, according to one of the SSP's central theses, the theoretician is not centrally relevant to theorization or to theories (see *SB* 2.3.2.5). Among the consequences of this thesis are that whether *SB* and *BG* author Lorenz B. Puntel or *TAPTOE* author Alan White or any other theoretician believes or argues or contends something or other is not of central philosophical importance, and that what *is* of central philosophical importance is the status of that something or other as a component of a theory presented in *SB*, *BG*, or *TAPTOE* (or elsewhere).

The second reason for avoiding speaking of the author of this book is a reason for avoiding speaking of authors at all. This reason is that authors often change their minds. It thus makes no sense, for example, to write without qualification about Hilary Putnam's beliefs about philosophical issues, because theses contained in his later works often explicitly contradict ones contained in his earlier works. The kinds of qualifications required are present in the following sentence: "In 'Time and Physical Geometry' (1967/1979), Putnam presupposes metaphysical realism, but in 'Sense, Nonsense, and the Senses' (1994), he rejects metaphysical realism." Sentences containing such qualifications can be important in philosophical accounts, but it is not important that they attribute beliefs or positions to authors instead of attributing theses or positions to texts. *TAPTOE* does the latter, relying on formulations like "Putnam 1967/1979 presupposes metaphysical realism, but Putnam 1994 rejects metaphysical realism."

To put this second point somewhat differently: no matter what Lorenz B. Puntel or Alan White may believe or indeed may ever have believed, *SB* and *TAPTOE* will continue to present the theories that they present as long as copies of them exist, and it is those theories—and not Lorenz B. Puntel or Alan White—that are the proper focus of philosophical attention. In order accurately to reflect this centrally important fact, *TAPTOE* speaks for itself, and allows *SB* and other texts to speak for themselves as well. Hence, the following sentence is true: *SB* often attributes theses and theories to philosophers—for example (84), "Quine presents," "Quine maintains," "Quine designates"—whereas *TAPTOE* (other than in 1.2) attributes them only to texts (e.g. "Quine 1992 argues").

1.5 The structure of this book

Following the preliminaries covered in Chapter 1, Chapter 2 introduces the abstract theoretical framework of the SSP, in the process explaining what abstract theoretical frameworks are and how they are concretized. Chapter 2 is a concise alternative to Chapters 1–3 of *SB*, and is presupposed by Chapters 3–8. Chapters 3–8 are sufficiently independent of one another that they may be read in any order. Chapter 3 greatly expands the brief account of the SSP's truth theory given in 2.5. Chapter 4 explains the SSP's definition of knowledge. Chapter 5 sketches the SSP's value theory on its most general level. Chapter 6 presents an account of human freedom that supplements the relatively brief passages on that topic included in *SB*. Chapter 7 sketches a theory of beauty that is an alternative to the theory introduced in *SB* 4.4. Chapter 8, finally, presents some aspects of the theory of being presented in *SB* 5.3 and Chapter 3 of *BG*, introducing and then relying on a refined language in order to articulate being more coherently and intelligibly than does either *SB* or *BG*.

2

Theoretical frameworks

2.1 briefly indicates why the SSRPP relies on the term "theoretical framework"; 2.2 further clarifies the SSRPP's methodology, first treated above in 1.3; 2.3 introduces and comments on seven of the SSRPP's central theses concerning theoretical frameworks; 2.4 presents the central components of a family of abstract theoretical frameworks members of which have been dominant throughout the history of philosophy, but that the SSRPP rejects; 2.5 introduces the most central components of the SSRPP's own abstract framework; and 2.6 explains how the SSRPP's framework is concretized.

2.1 "Theoretical framework"

Two relatively well-known philosophical terms with significations at least similar to that of "theoretical framework" are "linguistic framework" and "conceptual scheme." The SSRPP avoids those terms because they could be taken to imply, misleadingly, that the components of the relevant frameworks or schemes are, respectively, exclusively linguistic or exclusively conceptual. Although it *is* a thesis of the SSP that abstract theoretical frameworks for systematic philosophies include linguistic and what are commonly termed conceptual components—because, in colloquial terms, theories are collections of meaningful sentences—an additional thesis is that any presentation of any theory must rely on other components as well. The most important components relied on by the SSRPP are, in addition to the syntactic and especially semantic aspects of its linguistic component, its ontology (which identifies what it recognizes as beings or entities), its methodology, and its truth-theory, which makes fully explicit how its linguistic component relates to its ontological component or, colloquially, how its sentences relate to the world.[1]

One point of central importance that recurs, in various forms, throughout this book is the following: although it is common to consider such things as standpoints, perspectives, and even languages as *limiting* or *restricting* theoretical inquiry, theoretical frameworks—which, as just indicated, include languages—*make subject matters available* to theoretical inquiry.

2.2 The SSP as a network

What the SSRPP terms science has a relatively precisely identifiable point of historical origin in ancient Greece. Its first participant known by name is Thales, and it reached vital points of initial

---

[1] Its sentences are both *within* the world (better: they are within being, and are entities) and *about* the world (about being and, in most cases, about entities). More precisely, the sentences are themselves entities that express or articulate either entities, or being as such or as a whole. The distinction between being and entities is explained in Chapter 8.

culmination with Aristotle's *Posterior Analytics*, which shows how theories can be developed on the basis of axioms and deductions, and Euclid's *Elements* and Archimedes's mechanics, which present theories of just that sort.[2] As physics began to emerge as a distinct science, the need for axiomatization decreased in importance as increasing emphasis was placed both on quantification—reflected in Galileo's dictum that the book of the world is written in the language of mathematics—and on experimentation. Because however the subject matter for the inquiry that continued to be most central to philosophy—the inquiry that Descartes, following Aristotle, termed first philosophy—is not quantifiable and not available for experimentation, the axiomatic method so successfully applied in geometry continued for far longer to appear to be the only one available for it.

Presumably in significant part because of both (1) the success of Euclidean geometry and (2) philosophy's lack of identified alternatives to the axiomatic theory-form, throughout modern philosophy, philosophical theories have had, as their most prominent analogical counterparts, buildings having foundations. Conceived of in light of this analogy, components of the theories are supported (or grounded) by resting on previously supported components, down to the foundation that, in the analogy, supports everything else. Among metaphorical uses of relatively ordinary English that reinforce this analogy, in addition to talk of theses and theories being founded, grounded, and supported, is talk of their having groundworks, bases,

---

[2] See Wolpert 1993/1998: xii, Ch. 3 or, for a far more detailed account, Russo 2004.

and footings, and of their being undermined. Demands that philosophical theses be "proved" often also reinforce the analogy.[3]

TAPTOE avoids foundational language by using variants of the term "stabilization." In order better to stabilize that usage, this section identifies some of the flaws in the buildings-with-foundations analogy, introduces two analogies that avoid some of those flaws, and then clarifies the SSP as a comprehensive theory by means of theses drawn from consideration of those two analogies.

One central flaw in the building-with-foundations analogy arises from what can reasonably be termed its pre-Copernican status: a building resting on a foundation is a terrestrial edifice whose structural integrity can require but is also threatened by gravity, and is preserved not only (in some but not in the simplest cases) by its inner structuration but also (in all cases, ultimately) by the earth. The earth is presupposed simply to be stable, so even in uses of the analogy that recognize—as, for example, does Kant's *Critique of Pure Reason* (A5/B9)—that foundations must be laid on solid ground presuppose that whatever underlies that ground supports it.

A somewhat different way of articulating this decisive flaw in the building-with-foundations analogy is the following: the structuration of buildings with foundations presupposes ground (the earth) and

---

[3] A famous passage from Wittgenstein's *Philosophical Investigations* (Section 115) reads as follows:

A *picture* held us captive. And we could not get outside it, for it lay in our language and language seemed to repeat it to us inexorably.

The buidings-with-foundations analogy ("picture" or not) has held philosophy captive, in part because it is repeatedly implied by the English terms and phrases introduced in the main text. But, as this section shows, it is possible to "get outside it."

gravity, but because the SSP aims to be a theory of *everything*, there is nothing *outside the scope* of the SSP, so nothing analogous to ground for the SSP to rest on and nothing analogous to gravity to either threaten it or hold it together.

A first analogy that avoids this flaw is provided by D-Stix building sets.[4] These sets include colored wooden sticks of various lengths and flexible plastic connectors, each of which has several slots into which the sticks can be securely inserted. The stability of heaps of such sticks and connectors, like that of buildings with foundations, presupposes ground and gravity, but even the simplest of linkages, that consisting of a single stick inserted into a single connector, does not: the two components are stabilized in that they remain connected when tossed into the air.

As components are added to the simplest D-Stix structure, stabilizations of various sorts become possible. Adding two more sticks and two more connectors in any manner whatsoever yields a structure that is stable in that none of its connections depends on either ground or gravity, but that structure is made more stable if it is reconfigured into a triangle—it then also maintains its shape independently of ground and gravity.

---

[4] In the philosophical literature, the standard "coherentist" counterpart to the building-with-foundations analogy is "Neurath's boat," introduced in Neurath 1921 and made philosophically prominent in Quine 1960 (3ff.). According to the latter,

> We are like sailors who on the open sea must reconstruct their ship but are never able to start afresh from the bottom. Where a beam is taken away a new one must at once be put there, and for this the rest of the ship is used as support. In this way, by using the old beams and driftwood the ship can be shaped entirely anew, but only by gradual reconstruction.

Among the flaws of this analogy is that it remains pre-Copernican in the sense introduced above: ships are held up by the sea and held down by gravity.

D-Stix structures are of course constructed, and hence require constructors. There is however an important sense in which the constructor does not determine structural stabilization. The sense is revealed by an example: the most stable structure that can be made with six sticks of the same length and four connectors is a tetrahedron, and this fact is independent of any constructor. This is relevant to theorization because (as initially indicated above in 1.3 and especially 1.4) when theories are assessed, the most appropriate assessment is of the theories, and not of the theoreticians who formulate them.

The D-Stix analogy can also clarify the distinction between consistency and coherence. Any heap of D-Stix pieces is consistent in the sense that there will be no piece whose inclusion precludes the inclusion in the heap of any other piece, and that consistency remains unchanged if the pieces are heaped differently. As merely heaped, however, the configuration of the pieces is incoherent in the sense that no pieces are interlinked. As pieces are interconnected, the coherence of the configuration of pieces—the coherence of the structure—increases.

D-Stix structures, considered as analogues to theories, avoid some of the most important flaws of the building-with-foundations analogue, but one important way in which they are disanalogous to philosophical theories is that their components can be definitively determined: they include only sticks and connectives. A second analogy or analogue, which improves on the D-Stix analogy in this respect, is that of the space station. Components of space stations, like those of D-Stix structures, are not stabilized by being grounded or supported; the reason for this in the case of space stations is the at least frequent and possibly permanent absence of significant gravitational fields that those components must resist. The components are therefore stabilized, like those of D-Stix structures, by being interconnected. The components and their interconnections can be of various sorts and of various strengths. A wire that dangled loosely would be minimally stabilized; securing the loose end would increase its stabilization. Wires or girders (for example) connected to many other wires or girders would generally be more integral to the structure than would those with fewer connections, in that their disconnection or removal would destabilize the station itself to greater degrees. Correspondingly, theses within the network-structure of the SSP vary in status in that some are more tightly and multiply interlinked, and hence more central, whereas others are more loosely and less multiply interlinked, and hence more peripheral. Alterations to relatively peripheral components of the SSP could improve the SSP, whereas if superior alternatives to central components were discovered, the theory relying on those components would presumably be an alternative to the SSP.[5]

In addition, a space station, like a systematic philosophy, could qualify as the best available at some time, but not as absolutely the best; the possibility of superior alternatives could not be excluded.

Although the space-station analogy is appropriate to the SSP in ways that the building-with-foundations analogy is not, it is potentially misleading in one important way: space stations are situated within space—there is much that is outside them—whereas the SSP

---

[5] For specific identifications of some peripheral, intermediate, and central components of the SSP, see *Structure and Being*, Section 6.4.

is coextensive not only with the physical universe, but with being as such and as a whole (this coextensivity is considered in various places below, in *SB*, and in *BG*). According to the SSP being as a whole[6] is, as explained below (Chapter 8), the comprehensive configuration of facts identical to true propositions expressible by true sentences. To be sure, no presentation of the SSP could include all of those sentences (and thereby those propositions and those facts), but that is not because any of those facts are somehow beyond or outside of its scope. It is instead because human finitude precludes the possibility of any human being developing a comprehensive account of everything that is within the SSP's scope, and because the subject matters of the non-philosophical sciences are within its scope only in that those sciences themselves are within its scope.

2.3 Seven central theses concerning theoretical frameworks

Seven of the SSP's central theses concerning theoretical frameworks—theses that, as emphasized in 1.3 and 2.2, are in no way foundational—are the following (with "TF" indicating that the theses concern theoretical frameworks, and the theses themselves italicized):

TF1: *True sentences are situated within theoretical frameworks.* They cannot be situated beyond or outside any theoretical framework whatsoever, because—as indicated above in 2.1—they must

---

[6] Recent debates about issues in logic raise questions about the possibility of theories encompassing (in the SSP's language) being (or, in *BG*, Being) *as a whole*. These are considered in *Structure and Being*, Section 5.2.2.

(linguistically) express semantic contents (colloquially: meanings), and must somehow qualify as true. In the terminology of the SSP, the language in which a true sentence is articulated, the semantic contents it expresses, and the way in which it qualifies as true are components of a theoretical framework.

TF2: *Being*—which includes all that is—*veridically manifests itself—truly or genuinely reveals itself—within all adequately determined or determinable theoretical frameworks.* Among such frameworks are the tacitly presupposed and only vaguely determined frameworks that human beings rely on in their everyday lives when they are concerned with discovering and presenting truths—as, for example, when someone consults a newspaper in order to *discover* when the sun will rise the following morning, and *presents* the truth thereby discovered by uttering an indicative sentence, perhaps "Sunrise tomorrow is at 4:33."

TF3: *All truths are relative to the theoretical frameworks within which they are situated,* again beginning with the mundane truths that, like "Sunrise tomorrow is at 4:33," are situated within everyday frameworks. That sentence is of course not true within the framework of contemporary astronomy, wherein among the truths that are situated are that the sun is stable relative to the earth, and that the earth both rotates on its own axis and revolves around the sun. The two frameworks can be compared within a metaframework encompassing both; the comparison yields an explanation of why the earth, *although* veridically revealing itself within the framework of astronomy as moving, *also* veridically appears within everyday frameworks as immobile.[7] A consequence of this is that astronomers

---

[7] This example is reconsidered in 6.3.

can non-problematically, in their everyday lives, speak of the sun as rising and setting, as can non-astronomers who know enough about contemporary astronomy to be heliocentrists.

As is suggested by the example of earth and sun, the fact that being veridically manifests or reveals itself within all theoretical frameworks does not lead to any crippling relativism because, according to thesis 4,

TF4: *Within metaframeworks, apparently conflicting theoretical frameworks can be compared and, when comparison reveals the conflict to be genuine, ordered with respect to their theoretical adequacy.* In the case just considered, comparison shows that the conflict is merely apparent, so neither framework need be rejected. Everyday theoretical frameworks are more adequate with respect to everyday convenience and efficiency, and the SSP accepts those criteria as the ones appropriate for ordering such frameworks, but not as the ones appropriate for ordering scientific frameworks.

The SSP's criteria for comparing and ordering theoretical frameworks for systematic philosophies are relatively maximal coherence and intelligibility, such that the relativity is both internal (the superior account is more coherent and intelligible than is any other available concretization of its own framework) and external (the superior account is more coherent and intelligible than are concretizations of competing theoretical frameworks that are available).[8]

Although theoretical frameworks can be ranked with respect to theoretical adequacy, according to thesis 5,

---

[8] Determining the degree to which the truth of TF4 is relative to the theoretical framework of the SSP requires considering the relation between the systematic and the metasystematic levels of the SPP; see *SB* 1.5.2.2–1.5.2.3 and Chapter 6.

TF5: *No human theoretician could ever establish that the framework they relied on was the best possible framework for any sufficiently complex subject matter, definitively including the subject matter of systematic philosophy.* Establishing a framework as absolutely optimal would require identifying and comparing all of the infinitely many possible theoretical frameworks (or families of frameworks) for the relevant subject matter, and that, for human beings, is impossible.

From the conjunction of thesis 3—that all truths are relative to theoretical frameworks—and thesis 5—that human beings can identify neither all such frameworks nor any optimal framework—it might appear to follow, but does not in fact follow, that there cannot be or indeed that human beings cannot identify any absolute truths. The reason this does not follow is articulated by thesis 6, according to which

TF6: *Absolute truths are truths that have identifiable versions in all theoretical frameworks.* The most obvious such truth is the principle of non-contradiction, for no framework lacking a version of it as a component could qualify as a *theoretical* framework.[9] The reason is that within such a "framework," no definitive truths whatsoever could emerge.

A clear consequence of TF5 is that the SSP cannot include the thesis that its own theoretical framework is the best possible for systematic philosophy. It can and indeed does however include TF7—which, as indicated above, is stabilized in part by examination of alternative frameworks, either in isolation or in comparisons developed within appropriate metaframeworks:

---

[9]Determination that two distinct formulations, situated in different theoretical frameworks, qualified as versions of the principle of non-contradiction would require reliance on a metaframework considering both.

TF7: *The SSP's theoretical framework is the best that is currently available for systematic philosophy.*

One consequence of TF5 and TF7, in conjunction, is that although the status claimed by the SSP is in one respect highly ambitious, in another it is notably modest. It claims, ambitiously, to provide the best theoretical framework currently available for systematic philosophy, but it also anticipates, modestly, the future development of frameworks that will be better. It thereby claims for systematic philosophy a theoretical status in no way inferior to that of any of the natural sciences: those sciences, too, operate within the best theoretical frameworks that are currently available, but nothing precludes, and there are overwhelming reasons to anticipate, future developments of superior frameworks.

It is important to emphasize one additional consequence of the SSP's inclusion of these theses concerning theoretical frameworks. It is the following: the SSP is reasonably termed a philosophical theory of everything because its subject matter is the unrestricted universe of discourse. Within the scope of what is best termed its *systematic* level is, in a sense clarified above, everything, but *this* everything does *not* include theoretical frameworks or theories that are *alternatives* to those of the SSP. As suggested above, addressing such theoretical frameworks and theories requires development of and reliance on *metaframeworks*, which are developed on *metasystematic* levels of the SSP. The consideration, in the following section (2.4), of a family of alternative frameworks requires a step to a metaframework within which it becomes evident that the family is of frameworks that *are* different from the SSP's framework. The critique of that family of frameworks is an immanent critique in that it exposes problems inherent in members of that family. The next section (2.5) shows how the SSP's framework avoids those problems. The argument that the SSP's framework is therefore superior to the rejected frameworks is situated on a metasystematic level, because it requires considering both the SSP's framework and the family of alternative frameworks.

The point made in the preceding paragraph further clarifies the sense in which the SSP, if completed, would be a philosophical theory of everything. Its subject matter, the unrestricted universe of discourse, is comprehensive, but also incomplete in the specific sense that it continues to develop over time. The SSP does not ignore that development; instead, it explicitly acknowledges it. As a result, future theoretical frameworks and theories fall within its scope in that it explicitly anticipates their development. At the same time, however, no concretization of the SSP can anticipate, *specifically*, what theoretical frameworks or theories will develop in the future. This yields one sense in which the SSP remains an *open* system (see *SB* 20, 428): it is *open* to the arising of new theoretical frameworks and new theories, and *capable, as they arise*, of examining them. When, within a metaframework, a new theoretical framework or theory shows itself to be superior to the SSP, the SSP will no longer be the best available systematic philosophy.

This point may also be put in the following way: indeed, no concretization of the SSP can include considerations of specific, not-yet-available alternative theoretical frameworks or theories, but what prevents its consideration of them is *not* any restriction of its universe of discourse, but instead, precisely, the fact that they are not yet available. As they become available, they enter the scope of the SSP's metasystematic investigations.

2.4 A family of theoretical frameworks rejected by the SSRPP[10]

The theoretical framework of the SSRPP develops in significant part from the *rejection* of a family of frameworks members of which have been relied on, since the beginning of the scientific enterprise in ancient Greece, by the vast majority of theoreticians and—at least in much of the world—by human beings in their everyday lives. Showing that all members of this family are inadequate prepares the way for showing the superiority of the SSRPP's framework.

All of the rejected frameworks rely on more or less ordinary languages, such as English. Their components include semantic ones whose syntactic counterparts are subject terms (such as "Socrates") and predicates (such as "is a Greek philosopher"). The grammatical or syntactic subject most important to the semantics is the singular term taken to have a semantic referent whose ontological counterpart is a thing (or substance or object), such as SOCRATES. The grammatical predicate is taken, semantically, to designate what is, ontologically, either a property of that substance or thing (such as IS-A-GREEK-PHILOSOPHER), or a relation in which the substance stands to other substances or things (for example, IS-A-TEACHER-OF-PLATO).

That frameworks of this sort have dominated is not surprising, given their everyday efficiency and convenience. In their everyday lives, human beings find themselves surrounded by—to choose

---

[10] Throughout *TAPTOE*, the use of small capital letters indicates the articulation of ontological items (that is, entities); articulations of semantic items (concepts or propositions) are indicated by italic letters, and those of syntactic items (words, phrases, or sentences), by enclosure within quotation marks.

items now common in at least much of the world, and ones that have obvious counterparts elsewhere—such things as tables, rugs, oak trees, and Siamese cats, and it is non-problematic for human beings, in their everyday lives, to think of those items as things having properties and standing in relations to one another. Tables, unlike rugs, generally have legs, and the two often relate such that tables are on rugs but far more rarely such that rugs are on tables.

Everyday efficiency and convenience are wholly reasonable criteria for rating everyday theoretical frameworks, and frameworks relying (generally tacitly) on substance or thing ontologies often satisfy these criteria quite satisfactorily. Systematic philosophy, however, aims *not* at everyday efficiency and convenience, but instead at relatively maximal coherence and intelligibility, and frameworks relying on substance or thing ontologies fail to satisfy those criteria. They fail because substances prove to be *un*intelligible. According to thing ontologies, things have properties and stand in relations, but to have properties and stand in relations they must have an ontological status that is different from the statuses of properties and relations. One way to articulate that status would be to answer the question, what *is* a specific table, considered not as a table but instead as a thing? As a table, it has legs and is on the rug, but those attributes characterize it as the table that it is, not as a thing. The only way it could become accessible and hence intelligible as a thing would be by means of abstraction from the properties and relations that it has as a table, but the greater the abstraction, the less is left. Indeed, if the abstraction is complete, if no table-attributes remain, then there is no content whatsoever. The concepts *thing, substance,* and *object*, as components of thing or substance or object ontologies, are therefore unintelligible, in that it is impossible to determine or articulate what things or substances or objects *as such* could be.[11]

2.5 The SSP's abstract theoretical framework

The SSP's theoretical framework diverges from members of the family of frameworks just described first in relying not on any ordinary language, but instead on artificial, technical languages that both refine and expand ordinary languages (English, in *TAPTOE, SB*, and *BG*, German, in *Struktur und Sein* and *Sein und Gott*). The technical languages refine their ordinary counterparts particularly by disambiguating terms (such as "philosophy," particularly in the phrase "systematic philosophy"), and expand them chiefly by introducing technical terms (such as "theoretical framework" and "being").

Because—for reasons just indicated—the SSP's ontology cannot recognize things or objects or substances in any form, it also cannot accept subject and predicate terms as having semantic or ontological counterparts. Instead of relating its semantics and ontology to subject-predicate sentences, then, it relates them to the syntactic form of such ordinary-language sentences as "It's raining" and "It's morning," taking the "it" in any such sentence to be a syntactic placeholder required by English grammar, not a pronoun requiring an antecedent.[12] According to the framework's semantic component, sentences of the form "It's such-and-suching"—termed in *TAPTOE*,

---

[11] *SB* 3.2.2.3 (pp. 249–61) treats this issue in greater detail; see also 2.5.1, below.
[12] The "it" in such sentences is reconsidered in 8.3.1.

although not in *SB* or *BG*, "sentencings"[13]—can express semantic
contents termed "propositionings."[14] Ontologically, every true propositioning is identical to an actual facting, so that, for example,
the sentencing "It's Williams-Colleging" is true because—in more
ordinary language—Williams College is a facting that is a constituent
of the actual world, not of some merely possible world. Factings
are understood on the basis of the propositionings most intelligibly expressed by sentencings, that is, broadly, as happenings
(many of which are temporally extended, and many of which—
including ones in the mathematical domain—are atemporal). The
facting (for example) IT's SOCRATESING is an extremely complex one,
a configuration including among its constituents the factings IT's
ROBUSTLY-INDIVIDUALLING, IT's PHILOSOPHIZING, and IT's BEING-
AN-INTERLOCUTOR-OF-IT's-PLATOING,[15] each of which is itself
complex. IT's PHILOSOPHIZING is an example of a facting that can be
only as a constituent of an IT's ROBUSTLY-INDIVIDUALLING, and IT's
BEING-AN-INTERLOCUTOR is an example of a facting that is a relating,
such that it can be only as relating at least two robust individuals (two
members of the family IT's ROBUSTLY-INDIVIDUALLING).

Metaframework-level comparison of the SSP's ontology with the
thing (or object or substance) ontologies considered in 2.4 reveals

---

[13] See *SB* 15 and *BG* 184 note e.

[14] To decrease awkwardness, *TAPTOE* occasionally uses "proposition" rather than the
technical term "propositioning."

[15] More precisely, IT's SOCRATESING includes among its constituents members of the family
of factings IT's HUMANING and IT's ROBUSTLY-INDIVIDUALLING. IT's PLATOING includes
a constituent facting so highly similar to a constituent of IT's SOCRATESING that each
qualifies as an IT's HUMANING, but in the SSP's ontology, there are no multiply instantiated
universals. Hence, there is no universal IT's HUMANING, there are instead specific members
of the family. See *SB* 204, 213–14, 264.

that members of the family IT's ROBUSTLY-INDIVIDUALLING are among the factings whose counterparts in thing ontologies are things, that IT's PHILOSOPHIZING is an example of a facting whose counterpart in thing ontologies is a property, and IT's BEING-AN-INTERLOCUTOR, an example of a facting whose counterpart in thing ontologies is a relation. Centrally important among the differences between the SSP's entities and their counterparts in thing ontologies is that the SSP's do not differ with respect to ontological status, precisely because all are factings. Thus, because according to the SSP all entities—all beings—are factings, being veridically appears or reveals itself within the SSP's theoretical framework as the facting that is the comprehensive configuration encompassing all other factings (see Chapter 8, below, and *BG* 3.2), every facting being identical to a propositioning expressible by a sentence or sentencing.

The just-used phrase "sentence or sentencing" requires brief clarification. The SSP rejects the *semantics* ordinarily associated with subject-predicate sentences, but it need not reject sentences having this *syntactic* structure. To the contrary, subject-predicate sentences remain fully acceptable if they are understood to be convenient paraphrases of sentencings—again, sentences of the form, "It's such-and-suching." The reason is that what matters here is only semantics, not syntax. So, for example, a presentation of the SSP could include among its theses the sentence "All humans are mortal," but would understand the sentence not as saying that every substance having the property IS-HUMAN also has the property IS-MORTAL, but instead as being a convenient paraphrase of the sentencing expressing the propositioning *If it's humaning then it's mortalling.*

Because factings are identical with propositionings, the former are clarified by an additional semantic consideration. The semantics most intelligibly and coherently linked to substance ontologies, which are considered and rejected above (2.4), is, in one or another version, *compositional* semantics, according to which the semantic value (colloquially: meaning) of any sentence is a function of the semantic values (meanings) of its subsentential components. The essential subsentential components are subjects and predicates, but because subjects are taken to refer to things (or objects or substances), and because things (and objects and substances) are unintelligible, the SSP rejects the compositional semantics linked to subject-predicate sentences. It accepts instead a version of a *contextual* semantics, that is, one according to which words have semantic values (or meanings) only within the contexts of sentences. Also as indicated above, its semantics is linked to sentencings, which have no semantically significant subsentential components. In terms of semantics, any simple sentencing—any sentencing without operators or connectives, such as "It's morning"—consists solely of a verb.[16]

2.5.1 A further clarification of factings

Thing-based ontologies, if they could be made intelligible, might appear to be well-suited to account for what analytic philosophers

---

[16] Perhaps worth noting is that in some languages, including Spanish and Italian, grammatically correct sentences need not contain subject terms. For example, counterparts to "It's raining" are the Spanish "*Está lloviendo*" and the Italian "*Sta piovendo*." In ordinary English, the "is raining" of "It's raining" is the verb "rain" in the present continuous tense; this "raining" is not the gerund (as in, for example, "Raining turns to snowing when the temperature drops far enough") and not the present participle (as in "Raining from the sky, the bombs did enormous damage to the city").

often refer to as middle-sized dry goods, and to the so-called bodies of classical physics, such as planets and particles, but they cannot easily accommodate various of the entities that emerge within the theoretical frameworks of contemporary physics, including the likes of fields and collapses of wave functions.[17] Galen Strawson 2006 (28) emphasizes this point:

> The object/process/property/state/event cluster of distinctions is unexceptionable in everyday life [SSP: within everyday theoretical frameworks] but it is hopelessly superficial from the point of view [SSP: within the theoretical frameworks] of science and metaphysics, and one needs to acquire a vivid sense that this is so. One needs a vivid sense of the respect in which (given the spatio-temporal framework) every object is a process; one needs to abandon the idea that there is any sharp or categorial distinction between an object and its proper-tiedness. [18]

Having seen this problem, Strawson 2006 presents it as insoluble, holding that "We are as inescapably committed to the discursive, subject-predicate form of experience as we are to the spatio-temporal form of experience," and, for this reason, "discursive thought is not adequate to the nature of reality." Strawson 2003 (301) makes a related point:

---

[17] Chapter 8 shows that the subject-predicate sentences taken as semantically significant by frameworks with thing ontologies also fail to adequately articulate being.

[18] Significantly earlier, and following a different course of argumentation, Verdenius 1962 (333) draws a similar conclusion: from modern science, "the notion of substance has been eliminated, as a residue of infantile thought" (see also 333n3). Decades later, Ladyman and Ross 2009, *Everything Must Go: Metaphysics Naturalized*, reason similarly.

We face the fact that some of our most fundamental thought categories simply do not get the world right. When we think obstinately I think we can see a priori that this is so. But we cannot really liberate ourselves from the framework these thought categories dictate.

To Strawson 2006's contention that "every object is a process," the SSP replies that in its theoretical framework there are no objects, there are only factings, all of which are intelligible as processes, given a sufficiently broad understanding of "process."[19] Second, to Strawson 2006's contention that "We are ... inescapably committed to the discursive, subject-predicate form of experience," so "discursive thought is not adequate to the nature of reality," the SSP responds that its theoretical framework escapes that commitment, and that it holds that different theoretical frameworks are "adequate to the nature of reality" to varying degrees. Finally, to Strawson 2003's assertion that "some of our most fundamental thought categories simply do not get the world right ... [b]ut we cannot really liberate ourselves from the framework these thought categories dictate," the SSP responds that its framework, with its alternative semantics and ontology, is one not dictated by those problematic thought categories. Within the ontology of the SSRPP, no problems are posed by identifying such items as IT'S FIELDING and IT'S WAVE-FUNCTION-COLLAPSING as factings.

---

[19] All of the SSP's entities are "processes" in that all are engagements in being, or at work being the entities that they are; for explanation, see 8.3.1, below.

2.6 Concretizing the SSP's theoretical framework

In technical terms, propositionings are *semantic structures*, and factings are *ontological structures*. These, along with *formal or logical structures*, are the structural core of the SSRPP's abstract theoretical framework (see *SB* 3.2). Concretizing this abstract theoretical framework requires *reinterpreting* or *reconfiguring* what the SSP calls the grand datum. The grand datum includes the universe—or, in the SSP's term, being—as it is articulated in other theoretical frameworks, including both everyday frameworks and scientific frameworks. Items situated in other frameworks as things or properties or relations are, if incorporated into the SSP, reinterpreted or reconfigured or resituated as factings; what in other frameworks are situated as concepts are, if incorporated into the SSP, resituated as or within propositionings. Worth noting is that although the grand datum includes being as it is articulated in other available frameworks, it is not limited to being as so articulated; work within the SSP's theoretical framework can also thematize aspects of being that have no identifiable counterparts in other available frameworks.

Chapters 1–3 of *SB*—roughly the first half of the book—present the *abstract* theoretical framework of the SSRPP; Chapter 4 sketches concretizations of the framework for universal domains of the contingently actual dimension of being[20] (the natural world, the human world, the aesthetic world, and the world as a whole); Chapter 5 sketches concretizations of the framework for the absolutely

---

[20] 8.3.5, below, clarifies "contingently actual dimension of being."

necessary dimension of being (being as such and as a whole[21]); Chapter 6, finally, completes the presentation of the SSP's framework by sketching its various requisite kinds of metasystematic theories. All of *SB*'s and *BG*'s chapters also contain passages arguing that other available theories are less intelligible and/or coherent than are the counterparts of those theories contained within the SSP; all such passages are, technically, metasystematic.

---

[21] Chapter 3 of *BG* more completely concretizes the theory of absolute being whose starting points are presented in section 5.3 of *SB*. An alternative account is provided below, in Chapter 8.

3

Truth

The search for truths is older than philosophy, and the search for truth—the attempt to determine both what are candidates for being true (beliefs, perhaps, or sentences or propositions or theories) and just how it is that some of those candidates actually are true while others are not—dates at least to Aristotle. As with many philosophical searches, however, this one has not yet led to any widely accepted solution. The solution presented in this chapter aims of course not at widespread acceptance or even acceptability, but instead at maximal coherence and intelligibility within the theoretical framework of the SSP. By explicitly showing how the syntactic, semantic, and ontological components of that framework are interrelated, this truth theory powerfully strengthens the SSP as a holistic network.

3.1 clarifies the task to be accomplished in this chapter as a whole. 3.2 introduces substantialism and deflationism, the two most prevalent types of truth-theories defended at present, briefly indicating how the SSP's theory relates to them. 3.3 introduces what *SB* (2.5.2.1) terms the fundamental fact about language, which is, in terms clearly explained in that section, that syntactic correctness alone does not provide full semantic determination. 3.3 also shows how this fact undermines disquotational and deflationary theories of truth. 3.4 identifies the grammatical form of the truth term vital to the SSP's truth theory, a theory then presented in 3.5.

3.1 The task

The terms "true," "truth," etc., are ones that, like "know," "knowledge," etc., are used in ordinary language in a number of distinct ways, as is evidenced by the following examples: (1) "What he said is true"; (2) "The German Democratic Republic was not a true democracy"; (3) "I need to true the rear wheel of my bicycle." At the same time, however, within the scientific community (broadly understood), a single sense—one also relied on in many ordinary-language contexts—has long dominated the literature. Tarski 1933/1956 (155) phrases this sense informally as "*a true sentence is one that says that the state of affairs is so and so, and the state of affairs indeed is so and so.*" A clearer formulation is the following: "Sentence S is true if and only if (1) S says of a state of affairs that it is so and so, and (2) the state of affairs is indeed (in reality, in actuality) so and so." This is the sense centrally relevant to philosophy if, as in the SSP, philosophy is understood to be a strictly theoretical endeavor.

As indicated by the two formulations just introduced, albeit more explicitly in the second, a theory that adequately clarifies this sense of truth will require at least three components: a syntactic component, to clarify what items qualify as sentences, a semantic component, to clarify how it is that sentences can say of states of affairs that they are so and so, and an ontological component, to clarify what is or can be indeed or in reality or actuality so and so. The theory must also interrelate these components, most importantly by explaining how it is that states of affairs can both *be bespoken* (a matter of semantics) and *be* (a matter of ontology). Developing such a theory may of course require, in addition to adequately *explaining* the sense of truth introduced above, altering that sense in order to situate it within the theoretical framework of the SSP.

The ultimate task of this section is to present a theory that satisfies the requirements introduced in the preceding paragraph, but because of the difficulty and complexity of this topic, and because it continues to be extremely controversial, some situating of the theory presented here in relation to other types of theories currently defended is appropriate.

One way in which the theory presented here differs from other theories of various types is the following: this theory is presented as fully adequate *not* to everyday theoretical frameworks and thus to ordinary language, but only to the theoretical framework of the SSP.[1] This does not preclude the development of a counterpart theory that would be more applicable to ordinary language, but *TAPTOE* makes no attempt to develop one.

---

[1] The SSP's truth-theory interrelates true sentences and sentencings, propositionings, and factings, all of which are components of the SSP's theoretical framework, but not of theoretical frameworks relying on ordinary languages. Moreover, whereas within the SSRPP's framework propositionings are expressible only by sentences or sentencings, within everyday frameworks semantic contents can be expressed in many more ways, for example by gestures (such as nods or shakes of the head).

3.2 Substantialism and deflationism

At present, the most widely accepted taxonomy of truth theories distinguishes most broadly between substantialist or robust theories and deflationary theories; in initially adequate terms, substantialist or robust theories seek to determine the nature (or natures) of truth, whereas deflationary theories deny that truth *has* a nature (see Lynch 2001: 4). For present purposes, the only kind of substantialist or robust theory that need be introduced is the correspondence theory (of which there are various versions), because substantialist alternatives to the correspondence theory and also deflationistic theories tend to be motivated in significant part by rejections of the correspondence theory. Again for present purposes, the correspondence theory may be linked to the understanding of truth introduced above, that is, "Sentence S is true if and only if (1) S says of a state of affairs that it is so and so, and (2) the state of affairs is indeed (in reality, in actuality) so and so." This understanding appears to presuppose some form of correspondence theory in that it requires, for sentence S to be true, some kind of relation, loosely but at this point adequately characterizable as correspondence, between the state of affairs that S articulates and the state of affairs in the world. The SSP's truth theory retains the central insight behind the correspondence theory, that is, that whatever is true (sentence, belief, proposition, etc.) must stand in a determinate relation to what actually *is* (to the ontological dimension), but it denies that the relation is adequately articulable as one of correspondence between items whose ontological statuses are or are understood to be utterly distinct (for example, between beliefs understood as purely mental and thus as non-physical and worldly facts understood as physical and thus as non-mental). Also worth noting at this point is that the SSP's rejection of all forms of substance ontologies allows it to avoid the major objection to correspondence theories, an objection lurking behind the following passage from (P. F.) Strawson 2004 (452):

> What "makes the statement" that the cat has mange "true," is not the cat, but the *condition* of the cat, i.e., the fact that the cat has mange. The only plausible candidate for the position of what (in the world) makes the statement true is the fact that it states; but the fact is not something in the world.

Present purposes do not require clarification of how Strawson 2004 understands facts; the point important in this context is that whereas the ontological status of facts within thing- or substance-based ontologies can be (as for Strawson 2004) problematic, and thus a reason to adopt a deflationary account of truth, the ontological status of factings, within the SSP, is straightforward: according to the SSP, the *only* "somethings" there are "in the world" are factings, including various members of the family IT's CATTING SUCH THAT IT's BEING-ON-IT's MATTING.

Whereas, as shown above, correspondence theories can easily be linked to Tarski 1933/1956's informal sense of truth, and particularly to the reformulation of that sense introduced above, deflationary theories can be and indeed as a rule explicitly are linked to a formulation from Tarski 1944 that is—although is not generally seen to be—decisively different from the first formulation. The formulation in Tarski 1944, "schema T," is presented by (Hartry) Field 1972 (372), for English as he takes that language ordinarily to be learned, as follows:

(T)   *X* is true if and only if *p*

where '*X*' is replaced by a quotation-mark name of an English sentence *S* and '*p*' is replaced by *S*.

A standard example replaces the variables as follows:

"Snow is white" is true if and only if snow is white.

For reasons evident from the example, schema T is the basis for what is termed the disquotational thesis concerning truth: the sentence appearing in quotation marks to the left of the connective "if and only if," and there said to be true, reappears to the right of the connective, but without the quotation marks, thus as "disquoted." As Quine 1992 (80) puts it, "Ascription of truth just cancels the quotation marks. Truth is disquotation."

Why theories taking the disquotational thesis to be essentially all that need be said about truth are often termed "deflationary" is presumably evident: such theories let what they take to be the hot air out of theories granting truth an important role in theorization—often, the role of being the aim of theorization—leaving only the relatively trivial function of cancelling quotation marks. For deflationists, truth-talk is essentially no more than a convenience, making possible such locutions as "Everything he said was true."

Because adequate understanding of the truth theory of the SSP requires clear understanding of the inadequacy of schema T, and thus of all disquotational and hence deflationistic positions, that inadequacy is now to be demonstrated in some detail.

3.3 The basic error behind all deflationary theories of truth

Schema T, as presented by Field 1972, is strikingly different from the formulation from Tarski 1933/1956 introduced above in 3.2.1: absent from the second schema are any indications (1) that sentences can or (to be true) must *say* anything at all, (2) that it is necessary or even relevant, for truth, that states of affairs be said to be so and so, and (3) that it is necessary or even relevant, again for truth, that states of affairs *indeed be* so and so. Instead, Field 1972's schema says something that, put bluntly, is astonishing: the name of a given sentence—the sentence as enclosed in quotation marks—is true if and only if that sentence.

According to (Paul) Horwich 2001 (559), "the meaning of the truth predicate is fixed by" its version of schema T.[2] The schema cannot however "fix" the meaning of the truth predicate because—in anticipatory reliance on terms thoroughly explained in the following paragraphs—(1) the sentence (or, for Horwich 2001, proposition) appearing on the right-hand side of the equivalence symbol in any instance of the schema appears *without determination or qualification*, (2) sentences (and propositions) that appear without determination or qualification are *semantically underdetermined*, and (3) "fixing the meaning" of truth-language requires sentences (and propositions) that appear as and indeed (at a later step) *are* fully semantically determined. Why this is so is now to be shown.

---

[2] The differences between Horwich 2001's and Field 1972's versions of schema T are not relevant to the account that follows.

A convenient starting point for showing how sentences can appear both as fully semantically determined and as semantically underdetermined is provided by an example from Field 1972, an example that indeed Field 1972 itself explains only by relying on resources beyond the scope of those provided by its own schema T. The example:

> The notion of truth serves a great many purposes, but I suspect that its original purpose—the purpose for which it was first developed—was to aid us in utilizing the utterances of others in drawing conclusions about the world. To take an extremely simple example, suppose that a friend reports that he's just come back from Alabama and that there was a foot of snow on the ground there. Were it not for his report we would have considered it extremely unlikely that there was a foot of snow on the ground in Alabama—but the friend knows snow when he sees it and is not prone to telling us lies for no apparent reason, and so after a brief deliberation we conclude that probably there *was* a foot of snow in Alabama. What we did here was first to use our evidence about the person and his situation to decide that he probably said something true when he made a certain utterance, and then to draw a conclusion from the truth of his utterance to the existence of snow in Alabama. In order to make such inferences, we have to have a pretty good grasp of (i) the circumstances under which what another says is likely to be true, and (ii) how to get from a belief in the truth of what he says to a belief about the extralinguistic world. (1972: 371)

The first point to be noted about this passage is its italicization of the word "was": the friend is said to have reported "that there was a foot of snow … in Alabama," and the "we" of Field 1972—henceforth, "Hartry"—to have concluded that "there probably *was* a foot of snow in Alabama." The italicization is important because it is a direct counterpart to the "indeed" used in Tarski 1933/1956's informal characterization of truth, but absent from schema T. Schema T, as noted above, appears to support the disquotational thesis about truth because the sequence including enclosing quotation marks on the left-hand side of the equivalence connective differs from the sequence on the right-hand side only by its inclusion of the quotation marks. It is however essential to note that if either the "indeed" or Field 1972's italicization is required, then the schema no longer applies, because then the sentence on the right-hand side of the equivalence connective does *not* differ from the one on the left-hand side *only* by lacking quotation marks. For this reason, a distinction must be drawn between the *exclusively* disquotational thesis and *expansively* disquotational theses; the latter are similar to the former in containing quotation marks only to the left of the equivalence sign, but differ essentially from the former in containing, to the right of the equivalence sign, formulations that do *not* simply repeat the sequence appearing within quotation marks on the left-hand side. Again, examples clarify:

> Exclusively disquotational thesis: "Snow is white" is true if and only if snow is white.
>
> Expansively disquotational thesis 1: "Snow is white" is true if and only if snow is *indeed* white.
>
> Expansively diquotational thesis 2: "Snow is white" is true if and only if snow *is* white.

Although Quine 1992 is disquotationalist (see the passage quoted above), Quine 1970 clearly recognizes the importance of Tarski 1933/1956's "indeed:" "'The sentence 'Snow is white' is true, as Tarski has taught us, if and only if *real* snow is *really* white" (10; emphases added).[3] This yields

Expansively disquotational thesis 3: "Snow is white" is true if and only if *real* snow is *really* white.

Further clarification is provided by closer consideration of Field 1972's example, which proves to be far from simple. To be noted first is that although Field 1972 begins and ends by speaking of *utterances*, it also characterizes the friend's *uttering* as a *reporting*, and the utterance itself as a *report*. Having done so, it describes an inference not from *utterance* to truth, but from *report* to truth; the description thus ignores a step that must be made. The step Field 1972 misses is the step made *in assuming or deciding or concluding that the friend's utterance was (probably) a report* or, differently stated, in assuming or concluding that in *uttering* the friend was *reporting*.[4] Hartry makes

---

[3] In a footnote, McGinn 2003 cites Quine 1970's "real snow is really white" passage in support of the following (87): "Disquotation is the essence of truth. This much is widely accepted." Eleven pages later in the essay, there is the sentence "Falsity is not, strictly speaking, disquotational: we have the schema 'p is false iff not-*p*', and the right side is not a disquotation of the left, since it contains 'not' and p lacks this word." This same consideration obviously rules out "Real snow is really white" as disquotational of "'Snow is white.'" That McGinn fails to note this is evidence of the strength of the disquotational dogma.

[4] Quine 1970 (12) makes the same error in the following passage:

The truth predicate is a device of disquotation. We may affirm a single sentence by just uttering it, unaided by quotation or by the truth predicate.

The crucial word in this passage is "may." Indeed, we *may* affirm single sentences by uttering them, but not by *just* uttering them, because we may also utter single sentences without affirming them, as we do, for example, in pronunciation exercises in language classes, or when we are acting.

the step on the basis of "the circumstances under which" the friend was speaking, but *not*, despite the description's suggestion to the contrary, solely on the basis of "evidence about the person and his situation." The relevant evidence about the person identified in the example is that "he knows snow when he sees it and is not prone to telling us lies for no reason," and the relevant evidence about the friend's situation appears to be that he currently has no apparent reason for telling lies. *This* evidence is however irrelevant with respect to the determination of the friend's *uttering* as a *telling* or *reporting*. The evidence vital with respect to *that* determination is *the context within which the uttering occurs.*

The importance of the step that determines the uttering as a reporting becomes clear if possible variants of the situation are considered. What if the friend, no less cognizant of snow and no more inclined frivolously to lie, had uttered "I just returned from Alabama and there's a foot of snow there" while reading aloud to his children, or in the course of telling a joke, or while on stage, acting in a play? In those cases, the friend *couldn't* be *lying* to his interlocutors about weather conditions in Alabama because, although uttering the sentence in question—and indeed uttering it meaningfully, within the context of the story, joke, or play[5]—he would not be *reporting* anything at all.

Of the four kinds of utterings identified in the preceding paragraph, *only reporting* presents the sentence (or the proposition

---

[5] In such contexts, the sentence expresses a proposition; if it did not, it would be unintelligible. What it fails to do is to present the proposition as true. Van Inwagen 2003 (149n. 5) misses this distinction in writing that sentences such as "Mr. Leopold Bloom ate with relish the inner organs of beasts and fowl," in works of fiction, do not express propositions because their authors are not asserting them.

or belief, etc., that it expresses) as *fully semantically determined*. In Tarski 1933/1956's terms, only then does the sentence say of a state of affairs *that it is so and so*. And that is why that is the only one of the four cases in which the friend's knowledgeability about snow and his tendency not to lie become relevant.

The preceding paragraph tacitly identifies *two* ways in which sentences can appear or be presented as fully semantically determined. The first is explicitly (although, as indicated above, not fully accurately) identified by Field 1972 as relevant to its example; this is, to rely on some of Field 1972's words, "the circumstances under which" someone says something or other. This way or manner in which sentences appear or are presented as fully semantically determined is the one most common in ordinary conversations and in everyday life, in cases of both spoken and written presentations of sentences. It is here termed the *contextual* mode of presenting sentences as fully semantically determined.

In Field 1972's example, the context within which the friend spoke is sufficient to determine the friend's uttering as a reporting; but what if the example is altered once again, now in such a way that the context becomes insufficient? What if Hartry hears the sentence in question in relative isolation, from what is otherwise a buzz of voices in an adjacent room? Surprised by the utterance, Hartry *might* wonder whether or not there was indeed so much snow in Alabama, but he might equally reasonably wonder (and would perhaps more plausibly wonder) about the *status* of the utterance. If his wonder were of the latter sort, one reasonable step would be to ask someone who had just come from the other room something like, "What's going on in there?". Responses that would overcome his wonder would include "Joe's been reporting on his trip to Alabama" and "Joe told us a great joke."

Use of the term "reporting," in the preceding paragraph as in Field 1972's example, is an instance of a second way in which sentences can appear or be presented as fully semantically determined, that is, by means of pragmatic vocabulary. In addition to "report," such terms as "assert" and "maintain" can accomplish this mode of semantic presentation, here termed the *pragmatic* mode. This mode requires a language richer than that required by contextual determination, because contextual determination, while it is *of* linguistic items, is not itself linguistic (it occurs only when there are appearances or presentations of sentences, but it does not involve the introduction of new words or sentences). Moreover, pragmatic vocabulary makes *explicit* what is only *implicit* on the contextual level: it *makes explicit* that what Joe was *doing* was *reporting*; it makes explicit how Joe was *using* language.

If he concluded that the friend had been reporting on his trip to Alabama, Hartry might again (as before) wonder about the amount of snow in that state, but he might also reasonably consider, as in the example, the reliability of his friend. In the example, he deems the friend trustworthy, but what if he is not sufficiently confident about that? He then reasonably wonders whether what the friend had said was *true*. Articulation of this wonder would take Hartry to a third level, that at which *semantic* vocabulary—here, the word "true"—is available. And just as what remains implicit on the first or contextual level can be made explicit on the second or pragmatic level, by means of *pragmatic* vocabulary items, what remains implicit on the pragmatic level can be made explicit on the third or semantic level, by means of *semantic* vocabulary items. In *reporting to* his interlocutors, "I just returned from Alabama and there's a foot of snow there," Joe is *presenting the sentence as fully semantically determined by presenting it as true.* He can make this explicit by using the semantic term "true": "It is true that there is a foot of snow in Alabama." *Without* semantic vocabulary, it is impossible to explicitly articulate what one does when one asserts or maintains. Moreover, semantic vocabulary does not require pragmatic vocabulary; "It is true that *S*" can present *S* as fully determined.[6]

The sentence "It is true that *S*" can *present S* as fully semantically determined, but *S is* fully semantically determined only when, within the theoretical framework in which it is situated, it is situated either as true or as false.

3.4 The truth term

Considered in terms of surface grammar, the term "truth," as a singular noun, appears to refer to some thing or object, whereas the predicate "is true" appears to designate a property. Given that the ontology of

---

[6] For "It is true that *S*" to present *S* as fully determined, "It is true that *S*" must itself of course be determined. For this reason, contextual determination is in a certain sense ultimate, because if sentence-appearances could be determined only pragmatically and/ or semantically, any such determination would require an additional sentence to accomplish the determination, the latter sentence would have to be determined by an additional sentence, and there would be an infinite regress. In a different respect, however, semantic determination is ultimate, in that (1) it alone explicitly articulates the determinations accomplished on the contextual and pragmatic levels, and (2) there is no further level that would explicate it.

Contextual determination can be provided not only by conversational factors, as it often is in everyday life, but also by situatedness within a presentation of a theory. The sentences in this book are contextually determined in the latter manner.

the SSP includes only factings, and thus neither things nor properties, it clearly cannot understand the truth term in accordance with the surface grammar of either of the two linguistic forms just introduced. The form of the truth term it recognizes instead is its appearance in the operator "It is true that ..." *TAPTOE*, like *SB*, at times does use the terms "truth" and "true," but only on metasystematic levels—that is, in considering alternative theoretical frameworks, as in 4.2—or, on the immanently systematic level of the SSP, in convenient paraphrases of more cumbersome formulations using the truth operator.

3.5 It is true that ... if and only if ...

The title of this subsection is the framework of a schema that is an alternative to schema T. In all concretizations of the schema, it must somehow be made explicit that what appears to the right of the equivalence connective "if and only if" (symbolized in what follows by "↔") has an ontological status. *Structure and Being* introduces the following possible ways of making this explicit (adapted from 301):

(T')   It is true that snow is white ↔ really: snow is white

(T'')   It is true that p ↔ really: p

(T''')   It is true that snow is white ↔ **Snow is white**

(T'''') It is true that p ↔ p

Given the considerations introduced above in this section, along with the syntactic, semantic, and ontological structures presented in 2.6, the SSP's truth theory is relatively easily expressed by the following conjunctions:

It is true that S if and only if S is a sentence or sentencing that expresses a propositioning P and it is true that P.

It is true that P if and only if P is a propositioning that is identical to a facting that is a constituent of the actual dimension of being (or: of the dimension of actual being).[7]

A partial formulation of the theory of falsity is the following:

It is false that S if and only if S is a sentence or sentencing that expresses *either* (a) a pseudo-proposition[8] *or* (b) a propositioning P and it is false that P.

It is false that P if and only if P is a propositioning that is identical to a facting that is a constituent of the non-actual dimension of being (or: of a non-actual world, hence a merely possible world).[9]

The propositioning expressible by the sentence "Mr. Leopold Bloom ate with relish the inner organs of beasts and fowls" is thus false, although it is true—it is actually the case—that within the merely possible (or: non-actual) world presented in Joyce's *Ulysses*, Mr. Leopold Bloom eats with relish the inner organs of beasts and fowls.

The SSP's theories of truth and falsity relate syntax to semantics in that, according to those theories, syntactic structures (sentences and sentencings) can *express* semantic structures (propositionings). They relate semantics to ontology in that semantic

---

[7] Being and its dimensionality are considered in Chapter 8.

[8] "Fred drew a round square" expresses a pseudo-proposition; see 8.3.5, below (also *SB* 238).

[9] The sentence to which this note is appended identifies the most common cases of falsity; for other cases, see Chapter 8, note 25.

structures—propositionings—are *identical to* ontological structures—factings that are constituents of (dimensions of) being.

Worth emphasizing is that this theory includes an identity *thesis*, but is not an identity *theory*, because it includes the thesis according to which sentences and sentencings can express propositionings; the relation of expressing is of course not a relation of identity.

Traditionally, items that can be true or false in the sense relevant here are often termed truth-bearers, but that term suggests that truth is something like a property that can be designated by a predicate, and so is appropriate to the truth-theory of the SSP only if truth-bearers are understood as arguments of the truth-operator. The primary argument of the truth-operator, according to this theory, is the propositioning, because it is true that (sentence) S—the secondary argument of the truth-operator—if and only if it is true that (propositioning) P, when S expresses P. Nevertheless, the sentence can be termed the *initial* argument of the operator, in that propositionings are explicitly available only as expressed by sentences.

To say that true propositionings are *identical* to actual factings may sound strange. As suggested above (3.2), it would indeed be strange if propositionings were understood as somehow mental, and factings as being outside of the human mind. According to the SSP, however, being is intrinsically expressible and is expressible by language(s); language(s) can express being itself. Moreover, there is nothing puzzling even within everyday theoretical frameworks about the thesis that by means of language, human beings can present facts—that is precisely what witnesses in legal proceedings are expected and indeed required to do. What can make this identity thesis—the thesis that true propositionings are identical to actual factings—counterintuitive is the unclarity, within everyday theoretical frameworks as well as in many philosophical frameworks, of the ontological status of facts. If actual facts—as actual factings— are understood as expressible constituents of being, there is nothing at all problematic about the thesis that actual factings are identical to true propositionings expressible by true sentences or sentencings.

Being's intrinsic expressibility can also be clarified as follows. The SSP accepts as a matter of empirical fact that human beings, by thinking and speaking about being—or, more loosely, about reality or the world—engage with being in ways that exhibit high degrees of success. The SSP also accepts, as included in the best explanation of this success, that human beings attain it precisely by articulating being in its intrinsic expressibility—hence, that language (and linguistically expressible thinking) and being coincide precisely in articulation. To clarify by means of an example: one who denied that the attendees at the 2012 meeting of the Metaphysical Society of America had succeeded in assimilating facts about being (indeed, according to the SSP, factings constituting being) as they read announcements about the meeting, made inquiries or arrangements concerning transportation, and interpreted visual and auditory data provided by clocks of various sorts would appear to have no better option than to classify the presence of those attendees at the meeting as resulting from an enormous number of inexplicable miracles. The SSP defends its explanation as superior.[10]

---

[10] The currently most detailed version of this defense is in *SB* 5.1.

4

Knowledge

Despite certain problems with it (see 4.1), the definition of knowledge as justified true belief appears to be the one most widely accepted in recent and contemporary philosophy. The SSP's theoretical framework—along with a great many other frameworks (see 4.3)—rejects that definition. This chapter explains why (4.1), presents the SSP's alternative definition (4.2), and counters a possible objection (4.3).

4.1 The inadequacy of the definition of knowledge as justified true belief

Gettier 1963 (121) considers the following definition of knowledge as justified true belief:

JTB [Subject] S knows that [proposition] P if and only if

(i) P is true

(ii) S believes that P, and

(iii) S is justified in believing that P.

Gettier 1963 accepts the identified conditions as necessary, but denies that they are sufficient; to show their insufficiency, it introduces two of what have come to be known as Gettier problems, of which a great many appear in ensuing debates. An adaptation of one of Gettier 1963's runs as follows: Smith and Jones both work for automobile manufacturer Superior Motors, which makes clear to all of its employees that they should own only SM vehicles. Smith notes that Jones, who always drives an SM vehicle to work, regularly drives to weekend softball games in a sports car produced by an SM competitor. With some admiration, Smith concludes that at least one of his co-workers is brave enough to buck company policy, even if somewhat secretively. Smith believes this conclusion, and there is justification for that belief in his observations of Jones's behavior. It may however be the case (1) that the sports car in fact belongs to Jones's brother, who trades cars with Jones on weekends in order to have the larger storage capacity of the SM vehicle, but also (2) that, unknown to Smith, his co-worker Brown does own a vehicle produced by one of SM's competitors. In this case, according to Gettier 1963's analysis, Smith would accurately be said to have the justified true belief that at least one of his co-workers owns a car produced by an SM competitor, but Smith could not accurately be said to know this, because the belief on which it is based—that is, that Jones owns a non-SM vehicle—is false. Hence, Gettier 1963 concludes, knowledge involves more than justified true belief.[1]

---

[1] It is worth noting that in this example, as in Gettier 1963's own examples and in the Gettier problems that have proliferated in the literature on JTB, the notion "justified belief" remains quite vague. No doubt, Smith has some reason to think that the proposition concerning Jones's car ownership may be true, but if Smith simply assumes that the only

Gettier 1963 triggered extensive debates along a number of lines (see *SB*, pp. 139–40, 143–4). In none of these lines is Gettier 1963's condition (i) drawn explicitly into question; the debates develop virtually exclusively on the basis of the generally tacit assumption that that condition is non-problematic. According to *SB* (p. 140), however, an "astonishing aspect of this state of affairs" becomes visible if closer attention is paid to that condition: what is astonishing is that definition JTB is circular.

SB's argument that the JTB definition is circular is extremely condensed. *TAPTOE* includes a more extended account of this matter; one reason for this is that more detailed consideration of the issue makes explicit the central importance to it of the SSP's thesis that constituents of theories, including individual sentences, are always situated within theoretical frameworks. The more detailed consideration also shows that closer examination of tacitly presupposed theoretical frameworks can reveal problems that, without such examination, remain concealed.

What, then, are the relevant aspects of Gettier 1963's theoretical framework—or, more colloquially, of the context within which Gettier 1963's definition appears? Its theoretical concern (121) is with "attempts … made in recent years to state necessary and sufficient conditions for knowledge." As indicated above, Gettier 1963's central thesis is that the JTB conditions are *in*sufficient—that there are cases

---

possible or even reasonable explanation for Jones's regularly driving the car is that Jones owns the car, then Smith is simply being naïve. Leaving aside other possible objections, including the one raised in what follows in the main text, there is the problem that what counts as justification in the examples would not qualify as adequate support in scientific contexts.

in which all are satisfied with respect to S and P, but in which S nevertheless does not know that P.

What, then, is required for condition (i) to be satisfied? In considering this question, it is important to note that unlike conditions (ii) and (iii), condition (i) does not relate P to subject S. Condition (i) requires simply that proposition P be true; it does not relate P in any way to any potential knower, to any theoretical framework, or to anything else. This fact suggests a question: within Gettier 1963's theoretical framework, is it possible for S or for any other subject to determine whether or not condition (i) is satisfied? If it *is* possible, then the definition becomes applicable in a specific sense: subjects (including S) can use it to identify at least some cases of knowledge, some cases of justified belief that are not knowledge, and, according to Gettier 1963, some cases of justified true belief that are not cases of knowledge; in a technical term, the definition is then *operational*.

How, in specific cases, would the definition be applied? S seeks to determine whether or not she knows that P. She asks first about condition (i): is P true? If she can answer in the negative, then she has determined that, P being false, she cannot know that P. If she cannot determine whether or not P is true, then it would be fruitless for her to consider conditions (ii) and (iii), because even if they were satisfied, that would not enable her to determine whether or not she knows that P. But what if she can answer in the affirmative? In this case, she has determined that P is true. Having made that determination, it would be senseless for her to ask whether she believes that P, or whether her belief that P is justified. But what is the status of this "determination" of the truth of P? Having determined that P is true, S stands in a specific relation to P. Ignoring the broader context provided by Gettier 1963, one would say that this relation is that of *knowing* that P. Within the context of Gettier 1963, that answer is clearly circular, because then she knows that P if and only if she knows that P. The circularity is avoided if the relation of S to P is something other than that of knowing, but what other candidates are available? Possibilities include "seeing," "registering," etc., but any one of these alternatives would then have to be clarified, and if the clarification did *not* involve *knowing*, then the term being clarified—which would designate an apprehension of truth involving neither belief nor justification—would designate an epistemic accomplishment superior to that of knowing. This would contradict a central if tacit thesis within Gettier 1963's theoretical framework, that is, that *knowledge* is the condition of maximal epistemic success.

Might it then be the case that Gettier 1963's theoretical framework is one within which it is impossible for S or for any other subject ever to determine whether condition (i) is satisfied—that is, might it be a framework with both skeptical and what are commonly termed metaphysically realistic components? It would then be one according to which (1) S can believe that P is true and (2) S can be justified in believing that P is true, and (3) it is simply the case, independently of S or any other subject or any theoretical framework or anything else—albeit expressible in ordinary English—that P either is or is not true, but also (4) whether P is true or not is something that S can never, in principle, determine. Within such a framework—a bizarre and deeply problematic one—S could express her condition of maximal epistemic success by saying, "Well, I believe that P is true, and I'm justified in believing that P is true, and P either is or is not true, so if it's true then I know that P, and if it's not then I don't know that P." Within such a framework, the JTB formulation would not function as an operational definition, and so would not be circular in the way that it is within frameworks wherein it *is* supposed to be operational.

Is Gettier 1963's a framework within which the JTB formulation functions in this non-operational manner? There is precisely one reason for identifying it as such a framework; that reason is that if it is *not* such a framework, then—as demonstrated above—its JTB definition, taken to be operational, is both circular and extravagant— circular because condition (i) is satisfied, for S, only if S knows that P, and extravagant because conditions (ii) and (iii) are superfluous. On the other hand, reasons for *not* deeming Gettier 1963's framework to be such a framework are provided by many of its sentences. It begins, "Various attempts have been made in recent years to state necessary and sufficient conditions for someone's knowing a given proposition." The article does not qualify this sentence—or any of the indicative sentences that follow, outside of the examples—as articulating merely a justified belief that might or might not, although unknowably to anyone, also be true; it instead presents it as true. Moreover, in its examples Gettier 1963 clearly attributes to Smith the capacity to, in effect, know in certain cases that condition (i) has been satisfied, that is, to register truths: "Smith *sees* the entailment from (d) to (e)" (122, emphasis added), "Smith *realizes* the entailment of each of these propositions he has constructed by (f)" (123, emphasis added).[2]

---

[2] Also worth noting is that Gettier 1963's framework implicitly includes a close counterpart to the at best deeply problematic metaphysically realistic component of the alternative framework introduced above: Gettier assumes as a fact about the universe that proposition P simply is or is not true. The implicit assumption could involve something like a

The preceding paragraphs reveal that whereas counterparts to the JTB formulation could appear in some perhaps possible albeit deeply problematic theoretical frameworks, wherein they would *not* be operational and hence not simply circular, the fact that such counterparts could so appear in other frameworks in no way alters the status of the JTB formulation within *Gettier 1963's* framework, wherein it *is* circular.

4.2 The SSP's definition of knowledge

The heart of the problem with the JTB definition of knowledge is that it contains a condition—that P be true—that is utterly independent of subject S, but one that subject S, in applying the definition in any case in which the condition is satisfied, precisely thereby comes to stand in the relation to P of maximal epistemic success and thus of knowledge. The problem is solved by a definition all of whose conditions relate S to P. The SSP's definition (*SB*, p. 142) is the following:

(K) S knows that *p* iff

 (a) S believes that *p* is true, and

 (b) S believes that S's belief that *p* is true is justified.

TAPTOE adds the following clarification of (b): S accepts *p*'s truth without question or doubt, and resists opposition to *p*'s truth.

---

superhuman omniscient subject, who would know (1) that P is true, (2) that S is justified in believing that P, and (3) that S can never determine whether or not P is true. If this omniscient subject accepted the JTB formulation, this subject would know that S knows that P, although S could never know that S knows that P. Without some such metaphysically extravagant assumption, Gettier 1963's premise (i) remains at best unclear. Moreover, the omniscient subject's knowledge would have to be defined other than as JTB.

By definition (K), p need not be true in order for S to know that p—so, there can be false knowledge, that is, knowledge that p when p is false. In addition to avoiding circularity, allowing such cases increases the intelligibility and coherence of the SSP because of its linkage to the thesis that all truths are relative to the theoretical frameworks within which they are situated. Within the astronomical framework relied on between the naming of Pluto and August 24, 2006, it was true—and widely known—that Pluto was one of the nine planets in the solar system. Within the astronomical framework currently relied on, it is true, and known to many, that Pluto is a dwarf planet, and that there are only eight planets in the solar system.

4.3 False knowledge

The widespread acceptance of the JTB definition of knowledge suggests that, for many, the phrase "false knowledge" is an oxymoron. It could of course be the case that in the languages of many theoretical frameworks the phrase is an oxymoron; that would not prevent its being non-oxymoronic in the language of the SSP. If however it were the case that in virtually all frameworks other than the SSP's the phrase were oxymoronic, then it could be argued that the SSP's definition is arbitrary and idiosyncratic. If it were then it could, as SB notes (107), "easily give rise to misunderstandings and confusions." If on the other hand there are other frameworks, including everyday ones, in which the phrase is not oxymoronic, the force of any such arguments would fade. Presumably the most straightforward way to demonstrate that "false knowledge" is not oxymoronic in a significant number of other theoretical frameworks is to present a number of passages in which the phrase is used intelligibly and wholly non-problematically, drawing from a variety of genres and covering an extended period of time.[3] Examples follow.

Harper 1996, a work in economics, drawing on and referring to Boland 1982 (185), also an economics text, includes the following:

> (Unintended) consequences are not evidence of the actor's so-called irrationality; they are evidence that some of the actor's knowledge is false ... A decision can be mistaken but still be rational if, in light of the agent's false knowledge of the relevant features of the situation, the decision is consistent with the agent's goal ... Boland ... would add another requirement for rational decision-making: the falsity of the agent's knowledge must be unknown to the agent at the time of the decision. (41n. 19)

In Roche et al. 1999, a work concerning management, there is (307) the following:

15.13 FALSE KNOWLEDGE

There is knowledge and there is knowledge. The idea of knowledge implies something totally positive. But we must be able to

---

[3] It could be objected that in at least some of the following examples, the "false" of "false knowledge" is best understood as comparable to the "false" of "false friend." On this interpretation, just as a false friend is *not* a friend, false knowledge would not be knowledge. Four points suffice in response. First, the objection is telling only if it is presupposed that knowledge cannot be of what is false. Second, none of the cited texts makes explicit that this is how its use of "false" in "false knowledge" is to be understood (all appear to presuppose that the phrase is clear enough to require no elaboration). Third, at least some of the examples— including the one from Roche et al. 1999 and some from Thornton 1999—cannot be understood in this manner. Fourth, in all of the examples, "false knowledge" is most plausibly understood as referring to beliefs that, although false, are relied on without question.

characterize knowledge by a component reflecting its source. Uncertainty is intrinsic. It may be due, for example, to incomplete or missing records. It could be due to human factors such as faulty memory or intentional deceit. We can place knowledge on a scale with extremes being true knowledge on the positive side and false knowledge on the negative side.

Weiss and Hoover 1964, a work in education, includes (21) the following:

Remember the people who "learned" that tomatoes were poisonous? They learned it all right, learned something that was false, and behaved accordingly …. [A]ny number of persons could learn (verbally or mentally) that tomatoes were poisonous, but they learned false knowledge. All of their behavior regarding tomatoes was guided by a verbalism that did not tell the truth about the "real world."

Frye 1964/2000, a convocation address at Franklin and Marshall College, includes (323) the following:

The real meaning of tradition is learning from the past how to live in the present. And the real meaning of revolutionary action is learning from what could be to see more clearly what there is. It is in the light of that present vision that we apply our practical intelligence to the world. This is real knowledge, as distinct from the false knowledge that we get from news media, propaganda, and advertising. False knowledge acts on what we think other people think, or can be made to think. (323)

Not surprisingly, given its subtitle, Thornton 1999, *Plagues of the Mind*. *The New Epidemic of False Knowledge*, a book written for a general audience, contains a plethora of relevant passages, including the following:

> The average high-school student today knows more that is true, and less that is false, about the natural world than the most educated intellectual of seventeenth-century England. (xiv)
>
> The "horizontal" spread of knowledge, its dissemination through widespread literacy, universal education, and high-tech media of transmission, has *not* banished ignorance, false knowledge, interested error, or institutionalized lies. (xvi)

It would be easy, but pointless, to provide additional examples.

5

Theoreticity, practicity, affectivity

An important thesis of *Structure and Being* is that chronic failures to adequately distinguish between and interrelate what it terms theoreticity, practicity, and aestheticity have led to deep and lasting confusion concerning philosophy on the whole, practical philosophy (especially ethics), and philosophical aesthetics. *Structure and Being* aims to overcome this confusion by scrupulously distinguishing among kinds of sentences, and indicating which kinds can, and which kinds cannot, be components of philosophical theories. A second important thesis emerges from the examination of the kinds of practical and aesthetic sentences that can be such components: sentences of these kinds can be true, and they can be true because practical and aesthetic values are (in conventional terminology) objective rather than subjective in the sense that they are full-fledged constituents of being.

In this section, *TAPTOE* builds on but also diverges from *Structure and Being*, first in speaking of affectivity rather than of aestheticity. The use of this term builds on *Structure and Being*'s evaluation (308) as "basically correct" of Kant's thesis that "all faculties or capacities of the soul can be reduced to the three that cannot be further derived from a common ground: the **faculty of cognition**, the **feeling of pleasure and displeasure**, and the **faculty of desire**" (*Critique of Judgment*, 178). Elsewhere (274), SB presents as the "three most important" of "the *absolutely essential* [factings] that are absolutely necessary constituents of human being … thinking (reasoning and understanding), willing, and being-conscious." Thinking is clearly the counterpart to Kant's faculty of cognition, and willing the counterpart to Kant's faculty of desire. Being-conscious, however, is clearly *not* the counterpart to Kant's "feeling of pleasure and displeasure"; *TAPTOE*'s affectivity is. It is an additional necessary constituent of human being.

SB links aestheticity to beauty. According to *TAPTOE*, what are traditionally termed intense aesthetic experiences of beauty involve being pleased in a specific way, which it terms being callo-logically delighted (callological delight is considered in some detail in Chapter 7). Hence, what SB terms aestheticity is included within what *TAPTOE* terms affectivity.

5.1 Modes of engagement

Structure and Being initially characterizes theoreticity, practicity, and aestheticity as "three fundamental and equiprimordial modes of activity, engagement, and presentation, i.e., three dimensions none of which can be reduced to either of the others or to anything else" (27). These modes are later presented as the three essential ways that "the mind relates to the world" (308). Most regularly, they are termed "dimensions of presentation" rather than "modes of activity and/or engagement," but the presentations are initially described as made by human beings who act in the three modes: theoreticians who present theories, agents who present (i.e., perform) acts (see 99), and artists who present works of art. These dimensions are also, however, ones within which the world presents itself to the mind. *Structure and Being* need not and does not explicitly consider how these two kinds of presentations—presentations *by* human beings and presentations *to* human beings—relate to each other. Because of the differences that become visible when the two kinds of presentation are considered in conjunction, *TAPTOE* generally terms theoreticity, practicity, and affectivity *not* dimensions of presentation, but instead—fully consistently with *SB* 1.1.2 (27) and indeed with *SB* as a whole—modes of engagement.

Human beings engage the world and are engaged by the world in the mode of theoreticity not only when they *present* theories, but also when they *come to understand* theories, and indeed whenever they register or attempt to discover truths. They engage the world and are engaged by the world in the mode of practicity not only when they act within the world, but also when they are confronted with needs, opportunities, or obligations to act within it. They engage the world and are engaged by the world affectively not only when they *present* deeds or works that are pleasing or displeasing to themselves or to others, but also when they are pleased or displeased by any entity or experience whatsoever.

Human beings, when awake, are constantly engaged theoretically, practically, and affectively, in that they are always situated within being in a manner that they deem more or less intelligible, more or less good, and more or less pleasing. The greater the degree to which I deem my situatedness within being inadequately intelligible, good, or pleasing, the greater is the impetus for me to alter my situatedness by making it, respectively, more intelligible, better, or more pleasing.

Any one of these modes of engagement can be the focus of conscious attention, and more focused consciousness—heightened consciousness—of theoretical, practical, and affective engagement can be triggered more by the mind or more by the world. Heightened theoretical engagement is triggered more by the mind in the case of the biologist who embarks on a search for new species in a rain forest or of the sports fan who looks to the newspaper to discover the results of the previous day's games, whereas it is triggered more by the world when a biologist happens to notice a surprisingly diseased plant while walking to work, or when a sports fan happens to overhear a radio broadcast announcing that a star player has been injured. Heightened practical engagement is triggered more by the mind in the case of the person who sets out to make an omelet for breakfast, and more by the world when that person discovers that, contrary to expectation, there are no eggs in the refrigerator. Heightened affective engagement is triggered more by the mind in the case of the person who, seeking callological delight—seeking to be pleased by experiencing beauty— visits an art museum or reads poetry, and in that of the person who, setting out to make the world more pleasing, writes a novel or removes weeds from a garden. Heightened affective engagement is triggered more by the world when, no matter how otherwise engaged, a human being is pleased by the beauty of a sunset, a building, or a discarded plastic bag caught by the wind, displeased by the ugliness of weeds in a flowerbed, or saddened or elated by a worldly event.

Like their Kantian counterparts, theoreticity, practicity, and affectivity are mutually irreducible. Theoretical engagement can but need not be good for the theoretician, can but need not be ethically good, need not be good for one's health, and is always more or less pleasing to the theoretician. Theoretical engagement is not good for the theoretician so absorbed in research as to become malnourished or sleep-deprived, and it is not ethically good if it prevents the theoretician from fulfilling ethical obligations. Practical engagements can be good for the practitioner even when based on false beliefs, can be bad for the practitioner even when based on true ones, and are always more or less pleasing. It can be pleasing to have false beliefs, and to do things that are bad for one and/or are unethical.

5.2 Theoretical, practical, and aesthetic values

Within theoretical frameworks relying on thing-based ontologies, values are problematic. Hence, the following famous thesis from (John L.) Mackie 1977/1990: "If there were objective values, then they would be *entities* or *qualities* or *relations* of a very strange sort, utterly different from anything else in the universe" (38; emphasis added). The use in this passage of "entities" in disjunction from "qualities" and "relations" makes clear that Mackie 1977/1990 presupposes a thing-based ontology. Even if, however, values would be "very strange" within any such ontology, it is not at all strange, within various familiar frameworks including (for example) those relied on by gardeners and auto mechanics, to utter valuational sentences that, within those frameworks, express facts and are therefore true. Such sentences include "Receiving appropriate amounts of water and sunshine is good for tulips" and "Running without oil is bad for automobile engines." Within the SSP's theoretical framework, there is no problematic strangeness with such sentences, or with such ethical sentences as "Murder is ethically prohibited," a sentence stabilizable, within this framework, as expressing a propositioning identical to a facting that is a full-fledged constituent of reality.

SB introduces four centrally important kinds of values: semantic values, basal-ontological values, moral values, and aesthetic values.[1] Semantic values are clarified in Chapter 3; the other values are explained in what follows in this chapter, and Chapter 7 is devoted to beauty, the most important of the values classified by *Structure and Being* as aesthetic.

SB introduces basal-ontological values in its subsection on the human world (4.3.2), but indicates that those values are situated within the natural world (treated in 4.2). This is so because, according to the SSP, such sentences as the following can articulate basal-ontological values, and can be true:

It is good for the tyrannosaurus rex that the tyrannosaurus rex eats the stegosaurus.[2]

---

[1] Aesthetic (or callological; see Chapter 7) values are the only affective values *TAPTOE* considers.

[2] A propositioning expressible by the sentence to which this note is appended is the following: *It's being-beneficial-to It's-tyrannosaurus-rexing that It's tyrannosaurus-rexing such that It's relating-to It's stegosaurusing such that It's eating.* Or, to use factings: IT's EATING is (in this case) a two-place relating (a relational facting) one of whose relata is "IT's TYRANNOSAURUS-REXING" (a facting that is not a relating but instead what *SB* calls

It is bad for the stegosaurus that the tyrannosaurus rex eats the stegosaurus.

The preceding formulations presuppose two theses central to the SSP's theory of basal-ontological values: the first is that it is good to be—if it were not good for the stegosaurus to be, then it would not be bad for the stegosaurus to be eaten by the tyrannosaurus rex—and the second is that entities—most importantly, organisms—are good *at* being the entities they are to greater and lesser degrees. It is good for the tyrannosaurus rex that the tyrannosaurus rex eats the stegosaurus to the degree that eating the stegosaurus contributes to the well-being, or flourishing, of the tyrannosaurus rex—what is good *for* the tyrannosaurus rex enables it to be better *at* being a tyrannosaurus rex.

Human beings, as rational and free (see Chapter 6), are good *at* being human beings to the degree that they actualize their capacities for rationality and freedom, hence self-determination; it is thus also good *for* human beings to actualize these capacities. These goods are basal-ontological values rather than moral values because they are ones whose actualizations contribute to the flourishing of human beings. Whether human flourishing requires the acceptance of moral values, and whether, among those moral values, are activating capacities for rationality and freedom, are additional questions. The SSP

---

a robust individual, or a member of the family IT'S ROBUSTLY-INDIVIDUALLING) and the other of whose relata is IT'S STEGOSAURUSING" (a facting that had been a robust individual prior to its fatal encounter with the tyrannosaurus). Formalized, with "E" for "It's eating," "T" for "It's tyrannosaurus-rexing," and "S" for "It's stegosaurusing:" E(T,S). Adding $\textcircled{w}$ as a one-placed well-being operator, determinable either as It's-being-beneficial-to, hence good ($\textcircled{w}_G$) or as It's-being-detrimental to, hence bad ($\textcircled{w}_B$), and indexed to specific factings: $\textcircled{w}_{G/T}(E(T,S))$, and $\textcircled{w}_{B/S}(E(T,S))$.

answers both in the affirmative, but there are possible and perhaps actual theoretical frameworks answering them in the negative. One such appears to be the one implicitly relied on by Thrasymachus in Book I of Plato's *Republic*; according to that framework, humans flourish by being utterly amoral.

Because (according to the SSP) human beings flourish to the degree that they are freely self-determining, they do not all flourish in the same way (as opposed, for example, to oak trees, which all flourish in at least essentially the same way). But one condition that must be satisfied for any human being who is to flourish as a human being, and that cannot be satisfied by any other terrestrial being, is that the human being learn a language within what some of the best currently available theoretical frameworks treating this issue term the critical period, which appears to end around the time of adolescence.[3] One reason this condition must be met is that it is only by means of language that human beings activate the essential human capacity of being intentionally coextensive with being as such and as a whole.

In learning any language that enables a human being to be intentionally coextensive with being as such and as a whole, the human being becomes able to understand and to use moral vocabulary. This is so for two reasons. First, *TAPTOE* accepts as an empirical fact that all natural languages include moral vocabulary. Second, according to the SSP there are moral facts (factings). Given this, a human being whose language included no moral vocabulary could not activate the capacity for being intentionally coextensive with being as such and as a whole, because that human being would have no access to moral facts.

---

[3] See, e.g. Fromkin, Rodman, and Hyams 2011, 62–5.

According to the SSP, of course, moral facts emerge only within theoretical frameworks. Any human being who is to flourish as a human being will begin to develop a moral framework as soon as that human being begins to master moral vocabulary. The everyday moral frameworks that develop as human beings mature contain empirical as well as moral theses. Over the course of recent centuries, empirical theses according to which women and members of certain races are somehow less than full-fledged human beings have been refuted by empirical evidence, and this has contributed to significant changes both in many everyday moral frameworks and in many legal frameworks.

Developing an ethical subtheory for inclusion in the SSP is beyond the scope of this book, but it is perhaps worth emphasizing that the subtheory is one that would qualify, according to some other contemporary frameworks, as speciesist: according to the SSP, the ontological distinctness of human beings, as rational, free, and intentionally coextensive with being as such and as a whole, accords to human beings also a distinct moral status.

For reasons given in the preceding paragraphs, moral values enter the universe (or, technically, the contingently actual dimension of being; see 8.3.5, below) only with the emergence within the universe of human beings. Because they do, SB's treatment of moral values (4.3.1) is located within its treatment of the human world (4.3).

The ontological status of aesthetic or callological values is more complicated than is that of moral values. The reason is this: although aesthetic values are *revealed* within the universe only following the emergence, within it, of human beings, those values can be revealed to human beings only because they are *independent* of human beings.

Hence, according to the SSP, the beauty of a given rainbow is revealed only when a human being, merely coming to see the rainbow, is delighted by coming to see it. But the beauty could be revealed only because it was there. More technically: the revelation of beauty is the activation of a capacity to callologically delight human beings, but the beautiful being (facting) is beautiful by virtue of its being an integral unity of proportionate constituents—hence, it *is* beautiful whether or not it callologically delights anyone. Beauty is considered below in Chapter 7.

5.3 Sentences and operators

According to *Structure and Being*, theoretical treatments in philosophy of both practicity (291–3) and aestheticity (306, 309) suffer from deep problems that result from unrecognized distinctions among different kinds of theoretical, practical, and aesthetic (*TAPTOE*: callological) sentences. To make these distinctions explicit, the SSP introduces theoretical, practical, and aesthetic operators. In this respect, *TAPTOE* differs from *SB* by introducing a well-being operator, and by using somewhat different forms of the other practical operators and of the aesthetic operator.

(1) For semantic values, the operator is the theoretical operator, Ⓣ, read as "It is true that" or, equivalently, "It is the case that." This operator is introduced above in 4.3, and further considered in 6.3.

(2) For what *Structure and Being* terms basal-ontological values, *TAPTOE* introduces a well-being operator Ⓦ with three forms, each of which must be indexed to the facting whose status is articulated:

$\textcircled{W}_{G/f}\psi$, "It is good for facting f that ψ" (i.e., better for f that ψ than that not-ψ).

$\textcircled{W}_{B/f}\psi$, "It is bad for facting f that ψ" (i.e., worse for f that ψ than that not-ψ).

$\textcircled{W}_{I/f}\psi$, "It is a matter of indifference to the well-being of facting f that ψ."

In specific cases,

It is good for (the well-being of) the frog that the frog eludes the snake.

It is bad for (the well-being of) the snake that the frog eludes the snake.

It is a matter of indifference to (the well-being of) the water lily that the frog eludes the snake.

As indicated above, these presuppose that, at least for organisms, it is good to be: if it were not good for the frog to be a frog, it would not be good for the frog that the frog eludes the snake.

(3) For practical sentences, the practical operator $\textcircled{P}$ is adopted; this operator takes as its arguments sentences articulating human acts or states of affairs involving human beings, and has the following specific forms:

(a) The practical-deontic operators

$\textcircled{P}_{RD/O,}$ "It is rationally deontically obligatory that"

$\textcircled{P}_{RD/F,}$ "It is rationally deontically forbidden or prohibited that"

$\textcircled{P}_{RD/P,}$ "It is rationally deontically permissible that"

$\textcircled{P}_{ED/O,}$ "It is empirically deontically obligatory that"

$\textcircled{P}_{ED/F,}$ "It is empirically deontically forbidden or prohibited that"

$\textcircled{P}_{UE/P}$, "It is empirically deontically permissible that"

These make possible such formulations as "It is empirically deontically permissible in Alabama in 1830 that human beings own slaves but it is rationally deontically prohibited that human beings own slaves."

(b) The practical-evaluative operators

$\textcircled{P}_{RE/R}$, "It is rationally ethically right that"

$\textcircled{P}_{EE/R}$, "It is empirically ethically right that"

$\textcircled{P}_{RE/W}$, "It is rationally ethically wrong that"

$\textcircled{P}_{EE/W}$, "It is empirically ethically wrong that"

$\textcircled{P}_{RE/I}$, "It is rationally ethically a matter of indifference that"

$\textcircled{P}_{EE/I}$, "It is empirically ethically a matter of indifference that"

All sentences explicitly or implicitly governed by the practical operator can be included in theories. Theses central to the SSP's ethical theory would include ones governed by the operators beginning "It is rationally deontically ..." or "It is rationally ethically ..." Sentences governed by the operators beginning "It is empirically deontically ..." or "It is empirically ethically ..." could be included as examples, or could be included in theories about deontological and ethical values included in moral frameworks relied on at specific times and in specific places. What may be termed directly practical sentences, however, cannot be included in theories. These are explicitly imperative sentences such as "Don't lie!". To be sure, such sentences are included in some texts classifying themselves, and classified by some others, as philosophical. Given the ambiguity of the term "philosophy," emphasized above (1.2), this is not surprising and need not be problematic.

(4) For callological sentences, the callological operator $\copyright$, which takes as its arguments sentences articulating experiences, and which is indexed to the human being(s) having the experiences:

$\copyright_{B/h,}$ "It is as beautiful that human-facting h experiences the facting that"

Aesthetic (or callological) sentences of this sort can provide data for aesthetic (or callological) theories, but at the heart of those theories will be sentences articulating aesthetic *evaluations*, not ones articulating aesthetic *experiences*; this centrally important distinction is clarified below in 7.4.

The theoretical operator is *always* the ultimately governing operator, because only it makes explicit the semantic status of what it governs (see 3.3, 6.3, 6.3.1). It therefore need not be included within the scope of any other operator.

6

Human freedom

The introductory chapter of the anthology *The Oxford Handbook of Free Will* opens as follows (Kane 2001: 3): "The problem of free will and necessity (or determinism) is 'perhaps the most voluminously debated of all philosophical problems,' according to a recent history of philosophy [Matson and Fogelin 1987: 158]." Kane 2001 continues:

> This situation has not changed at the end of the twentieth century and the beginning of the new millennium. Indeed, debates about free will have become more voluminous in the past century, especially in the latter half of it—so much so that it has become difficult to keep up with the latest developments.

Kane 2001 aims to be a "remedy" for those who want to keep up, but much of course has been published since it appeared. There can thus be no question here of presenting a survey of the immense literature on the subject, but neither the systematic character of this account nor the method of the SSP requires any such survey.[1] What the

---

[1] Kane's "Introduction: The Contours of Contemporary Free Will Debates" (2001: 3-41) and *A Contemporary Introduction to Free Will* (2005) are informative resources.

SSP's method does require is indicated below (6.2), following some
clarifications of terminology (6.1).

6.1 Terminological clarifications

(Peter) van Inwagen 2008a proposes (329–30) the following series
of "definitions" as ones that "serve to explain the system of concepts
everyone who thinks about the free-will problem should use":

> *The free-will thesis* is the thesis that we are sometimes in the
> following position with respect to a contemplated future act: we
> simultaneously have both the following abilities: the ability to
> perform that act and the ability to refrain from performing that
> act ....
>
> *Determinism* is the thesis that the past and the laws of nature
> together determine, at every moment, a unique future.[2] (The
> denial of determinism is indeterminism.)
>
> *Compatibilism* is the thesis that determinism and the free-will
> thesis could both be true. (And *incompatibilism* is the denial of
> compatibilism.)
>
> *Libertarianism* is the conjunction of the free-will thesis and incom-
> patibilism. (Libertarianism thus entails indeterminism.)
>
> *Hard determinism* is the conjunction of determinism and

---

[2] Formulations of determinism need not be as scientistic as is van Inwagen 2008a's; alternatives could ascribe determination to, for example, God or fate (see Kane 2005: 5–6).
Because the SSP rejects all forms of determinism (see 6.3, below), this qualification is not
centrally relevant here.

incompatibilism. (Hard determinism thus entails the denial of the free-will thesis.)

Soft determinism is the conjunction of determinism and the free-will thesis. (Soft determinism thus entails compatibilism.) (emphases added and formatting altered)

To these may be added the following, which characterizes a position defended particularly in numerous works by Galen Strawson:

Anti-libertarianism is the denial of the free-will thesis (both in conjunction with determinism and in conjunction with indeterminism).

6.2 Adding a theory of human freedom to the SSP

The SSP's method allows *TAPTOE* to develop a theory of human freedom by accomplishing three tasks (which need not be tackled wholly sequentially).[3] The first task is that of introducing relevant theses and subtheories from the SSP as presented in *SB*. The second task is that of integrating these theses and subtheories into an informal theory, adding theses, arguments, and (if needed) subtheories in order to attain relatively maximal coherence and intelligibility. The third step is in part metasystematic; it involves examining alternative

---

[3] The tasks identified in this paragraph do not correspond directly to the stages in the SSP's method (see *SB*: 41-52), but, as *SB* emphasizes (138ff.), those stages need not all be fully accomplished, and indeed can be fully accomplished only for relatively few subtheories within the SSP.

theoretical frameworks, including everyday ones, in search of truth candidates whose transformative incorporation into the SSP would increase its coherence and intelligibility, and of ones that, if left unchallenged, could threaten the SSP's claim that its theory of human freedom is the best that is currently available.[4]

6.3 A theory of freedom for the SSP

SB 4.3.2.5, "The Ontological Status of Moral-Ontological Values," introduces as there presupposed the thesis "that human beings as moral beings are free in the strong sense" (304), a sense that "excludes any compatibility with any form of determinism" (304n. 35). *SB's* position on the issue of human freedom is thus libertarian.

SB 4.5.3.4, "Does World History Have a Meaning," includes the following argument against determinism:

As a rule, we—we normal human beings, we individuals, politicians, teachers, etc.—daily live in situations within which we have to make decisions on which, at times, a great deal depends, concerning both our own lives and the lives of others. Assume that we understood the [physically deterministic] M-theory[5] and accepted it unrestrictedly. What effect would this have on us in the specific situations in which we would continue to find

---

[4]Important to its claim to being the best available is its being situated within an adequately articulated systematic framework.

[5]That M-theory is either deterministic (as it is presented in the paragraph to which this note is appended) or anti-libertarian (as is recognized in the following paragraph) is the only aspect of it relevant to *TAPTOE*.

ourselves? We would then *know* that everything, including the acts that follow our decisions, is always already governed by laws discovered by natural science. We would be faced with decisions, but would "know" that those decisions and the acts ensuing on them would be "governed" not by us but by purely physical processes. What *sense* would it then make for us to act? If we knew in advance that our acts had complete natural-scientific explanations, then decisions would be pure illusions, albeit illusions that themselves would be explained fully by the M-theory. If we were convinced of that—if we knew that—then all talk of freedom and responsibility would be nonsense, mere blather. What this shows is the following: confronted with the unavoidability of deciding to do one thing or another, we would all, in practice, reject or indeed refute, *by our acts*, the thus-understood, putatively all-explaining M-theory.

This would be the case even if one acknowledged that the M-theory did not exclude various indeterminacies …, because such indeterminacies would in no way suffice to make intelligible or to do justice to the (usually daily) situations within which we have to make decisions. The reason is that such indeterminacies cannot explain the basic fact that the decisions are *our* decisions, for which we are responsible—they are not the result of chance occurrences, however they may be understood, because if they were, they simply would not be *ours*. (344–5)

This argument involves on the one hand a family of theoretical frameworks members of which are relied on by human beings in their everyday lives, and on the other the framework utilized in

(Stephen) Hawking 2001, *The Universe in a Nutshell*. For the SSP, everyday frameworks are important sources of truth candidates, and include some truth candidates, the propositions expressed by what it calls immediate sentences, that are "absolutely indisputable" (*SB* 273). *SB* includes the examples "I'm thinking" and "I'm awake" (272), but to these may be added, "I'm trying to decide what to do" (or: "I'm deliberating") and "I've decided to cut class today." Moreover, a thesis included in the argument introduced above is that human beings often *cannot avoid* deliberating, that is, trying to decide what to do.

(Richard) Taylor 1961/1992 clarifies deliberation (41–2) as follows:

Whenever I deliberate ..., I find that I make certain presuppositions, whether I actually think of them or not. That is, I assume that certain things are true, certain things which are such that, if I thought they were not true, it would be impossible for me to deliberate at all. Some of these can be listed as follows:

First, I find that I can deliberate only about my own behavior and never about the behavior of another ....

Second, I find that I can deliberate only about future things, never things past or present ....

Third, I cannot deliberate about what I shall do if I already know what I am going to do ....

And finally, I cannot deliberate about what to do, even though I may not know what I am going to do, unless I believe that it is up to me what I am going to do. If I am within the power of another person, or at the mercy of circumstances over which I have no control, then, although I may have no idea what I am going to do, I cannot deliberate about it. I can only wait and see.

This accurate account of everyday deliberation, in conjunction with the unavoidability of deliberation, makes clear that everyday frameworks must be libertarian. An example clarifies. Presumably, for the vast majority of human beings it is impossible to deliberate about whether or not the sun will rise tomorrow, although it is of course possible to think about that. The reason deliberation is impossible is that according to the everyday frameworks most humans rely on, the sun's rising or not rising is, in the language of Taylor 1961/1992, a matter of circumstances beyond human control.[6] Any human being relying on an everyday framework including a governing thesis according to which *everything* that happens is beyond human control—any according to which, again in the language of Taylor 1961/1992, nothing is up to the human being relying on that framework—would be unable to deliberate. To be sure, a given human being might claim to be a determinist, but if that human being also engaged in deliberation, that engagement would reveal that the deterministic thesis played no governing role, precisely because if it did play such a role, it would make deliberation impossible.

That everyday frameworks are libertarian is a thesis a version of which is included even in the anti-libertarian works of Galen Strawson, many of which include the following example:

Suppose you set off for a shop on the evening of a national holiday, intending to buy a cake with your last ten pound note. On the

---

[6] Exceptional frameworks are not impossible. Near the end of the film *Black Orpheus*, the young boys Benedeto and Zeca rely on a framework that includes the theses that the sun's rising in the past has depended on Orpheus's guitar-playing, and that Orpheus, now dead, is unable to play his guitar. Deliberation leads to Zeca's playing the guitar; as he does so, the sun rises. The boys' deliberation presupposes their acceptance of the theses that the sun's rising at least may be up to them, and that playing or not playing the guitar *is* up to Zeca.

steps of the shop someone is shaking an Oxfam tin. You stop, and it seems completely clear to you that it is entirely up to you what you do next. That is, it seems to you that you are truly, radically free to choose, in such a way that you will be ultimately morally responsible for whatever you do choose. Even if you believe that determinism is true, and that you will in five minutes time be able to look back and say that what you did was determined, this does not seem to undermine your sense of the absoluteness and inescapability of your freedom, and of your moral responsibility for your choice. The same seems to be true even if you accept the validity of the Basic Argument[7] ..., which concludes that one cannot be in any way ultimately responsible for the way one is and decides. In both cases, it remains true that as one stands there, one's freedom and true moral responsibility seem obvious and absolute to one. (2008: 322–3)

The argument from *SB* introduced above includes the following premise: "Assume that we understood the [physically deterministic] M-theory and accepted it unrestrictedly." An individual's accepting this theory *unrestrictedly* would require *not only* accepting it as a component of a theory in physics, but *in addition* incorporating versions of it into *every* theoretical framework the individual relied on, including the individual's everyday framework(s). But given the unavoidable (if perhaps often implicit) inclusion of libertarian theses in everyday frameworks, such incorporation is *impossible*. Hence, "we would all, in practice, reject or indeed refute, *by our*

---

[7] The Basic Argument is considered in 6.3.1.2, below.

acts, the thus-understood, putatively all-explaining M-theory." The refutation is *practical* in the following sense: as Taylor 1961/1992 emphasizes, one who genuinely accepted determinism—rather than merely verbally espousing it—would be *unable* to deliberate. *That* human beings engage in *acts of deliberating* thus establishes that they *accept* libertarianism.

An additional question is the following: what if the acceptance of the M-theory was *not* unrestricted—that is, what if the M-theory was accepted as true only relative to a theoretical framework for physical cosmology? Or, more technically: what results from comparison, within metaframeworks, of everyday libertarian frameworks to non-everyday frameworks, such as that of Hawking 2001, which include deterministic or other anti-libertarian theses? The SSP's answer is clear: given its thesis that being is universally intelligible, the SSP cannot accept theses that comparisons within metaframeworks reveal to be inconsistent. Such comparison reveals the libertarian thesis to be incompatible with any anti-libertarian thesis, and hence any deterministic thesis. Hence, either the libertarian thesis, or all anti-libertarian and deterministic theses, must be rejected. The libertarian thesis cannot be rejected, so the anti-libertarian and deterministic theses must be rejected.[8]

The unavoidable inconsistency between the determinism or anti-libertarianism of any non-everyday theoretical framework

---

[8] From this it does not follow that, according to the SSP, all theoretical frameworks must explicitly include libertarian theses. Every investigation with a restricted universe of discourse excludes various topics; human freedom can of course be one of them. Hence, for example, a theory in physics with a deterministic thesis would, according to the SSP, leave out of its consideration the fact that human beings are free.

and the libertarianism of everyday frameworks can be clarified by consideration of two (among enormously many) merely apparent interframework inconsistencies that, because merely apparent, are in no way problematic. The first is introduced above (2.3) in clarification of the SSP's central theses concerning theoretical frameworks: according to everyday frameworks the sun rises and sets every day, whereas according to the currently best astronomical frameworks the sun is stable relative to the earth, and the earth rotates around its own axis and revolves around the sun. Comparison of these theses within a metaframework reveals that the everyday thesis can non-problematically be understood as the thesis that the sun changes its position relative to human beings on earth independently of the movements made by those human beings. This is fully consistent with the thesis that this change in position is best explained as contemporary astronomy explains it.

A second example: according to common everyday frameworks, the water poured into a glass is liquid, and the glass into which it is poured is solid. According to contemporary science, however, not only is the glass composed more of energy and perhaps space than of anything that could qualify as solid, but even on the macroscopic level glass—according to some theories—is not solid, but is instead, like toothpaste and shaving cream, a soft condensed material. Comparison of these theses within a metaframework reveals that the everyday theses can non-problematically be understood as involving the theses that when poured into a glass, water changes its shape and the glass doesn't, and that the water doesn't leak out of the glass. These theses, like the ones about sun and earth, are fully consistent with the theses that both glass and water are composed of bosons and fermions, and that the glass is a soft condensed material that is stable enough to hold water, to be held and drunk from, and to survive repeated washings.

Metaframework comparison allows no such reconciliation of the libertarian thesis with any determinism or anti-libertarianism, so inconsistency is avoided only if one of them is rejected. Again: the libertarian thesis cannot be rejected, because human beings cannot avoid deliberating, so determinisms and anti-libertarianisms must be rejected.

An additional argument included in *SB* adds another facet to its case against determinism. *SB* (353n. 55) relies on the following formulation, from Nagel 1987's consideration (135–6) of deterministic explanations of human reasoning:

> I have to be able to believe that the evolutionary explanation is consistent with the proposition that I follow the rules of logic because they are correct—not *merely* because I am biologically programmed to do so. But to believe that, I have to be justified independently in believing that they *are* correct. And this I cannot be merely on the basis of my contingently actual psychological disposition, together with the hypothesis that it is the product of natural selection. I can have no justification for trusting reason as a capacity I have as a consequence of natural selection, unless I am justified in trusting it simply in itself—that is, believing what it *tells* me, in virtue of the *contents* of the arguments it delivers.

A different way to reach a conclusion highly similar to Nagel 1987's is by considering the issue of semantic determination, introduced above in 3.3. Nagel 1987 considers a position according to which the semantic status of any sentence expressing something any given human being believed would be made explicit by the prefixing of the operator, "I am biologically programmed[9] to believe that ...." One sentence one accepting this position would accept as expressing one of their beliefs would be the following:

(S)   All my beliefs result exclusively from biological programming.

The semantic status of (S) is underdetermined unless it can be made explicit by the prefixing of the restricted biological-programming operator, as in the following sentence:

(S′)   I am biologically programmed to believe that
         all my beliefs result exclusively from biological programming.

(S′) is of course itself an indicative sentence. Because it is, its semantic status is underdetermined unless it can be made explicit by the following:

(S″)   I am biologically programmed to believe that
         I am biologically programmed to believe that
         all my beliefs result exclusively from biological programming.

(S″), like every sentence governed by the restricted biological-programming operator, is an indicative sentence whose semantic status is underdetermined, according to the position under consideration, unless it can be made explicit by the prefixing of that operator. The result, obviously, is an infinite regress. The regress is avoided only by the inclusion of the unrestricted theoretical operator "It is true that" (or an equivalent formulation).

---

[9] Here, "biologically programmed" means, roughly, that beliefs result from collections of purely physical events, including events within the brain.

What then about what might be expressed by an utterance of the sentence "It is true that all my beliefs result exclusively from biological programming"? In this case, the theoretical operator cannot stop the regress, because its argument, in this sentence, requires that its *ultimately* governing operator be the biological-programming operator. Because of its *argument*, the sentence could be determined as presenting a proposition as true *only* by the sentence, "I am biologically programmed to believe that it is true that all my beliefs result from biological programming," but the operator governing that sentence brings with it the infinite regress described above.

There is an additional relevant point relating to the passage introduced above from Nagel 1987. That passage suggests that human reasoning consists exclusively in following the rules of logic. The SSP emphasizes that such forms of reasoning as inferences to the best explanation or systematization, for example, require extralogical considerations (see *SB*, 43–4). More broadly: according to the SSP, *all* theoretical frameworks human beings *actually rely on when theorizing* must include, explicitly or implicitly, modes of what are often termed *inconclusive* or *plausible* reasoning, including reasoning concerning how to proceed. Because this is the case, all theoreticians, *when engaged in theoretical activity*, must deliberate. They must at times deliberate about which lines of inquiry to pursue, how to set up experiments, how to formulate their results, and so forth. For just that reason, the frameworks *on which they rely as they theorize* are libertarian frameworks.[10] As a result, the libertarian thesis is an

---

[10] Ironically, the facts that human beings are *not* free to include deterministic or antilibertarian theses within theoretical frameworks on which they rely when theorizing, and often *not* free *not* to deliberate, contribute to stabilizing the truth of libertarianism.

absolute truth precisely in that a version of it is at least implicitly included in any theoretical framework that can be relied on.

6.3.1 Responses to some objections from the literature

6.3.1.1 Taylor 1961/1992

Taylor 1961/1992 argues that both determinism and what it calls simple indeterminism, according to which some events occur at random, are inconsistent with the libertarian data introduced above (6.3). It restates (49) those data as including the following two theses: "(1) that my behavior is sometimes the outcome of deliberation, and (2) that in these and other cases it is sometimes up to me what I do." The work argues as well that the only position consistent with these data is (although it does not use the term) libertarianism. In its words (51):

> The only conception of action that accords with our data is one according to which people ... are sometimes, but of course not always, self-determining beings; that is, beings that are sometimes the causes of their own behavior. In the case of an action that is free, it must not only be such that it is caused by the agent who performs it, but also that no antecedent conditions were sufficient for his performing just that action. In the case of an action that is both free and rational, it must be such that the agent who performed it did so for some reason, but this reason cannot have been the cause of it.

The work asserts that "this conception fits what people take themselves to be," but then raises the following objections:

this conception of activity, and of an agent who is the cause of it, involves two rather strange metaphysical notions that are never applied elsewhere in nature. The first is that of a *self* or *person*—for example, a man—who is not merely a collection of things or events, but a self-moving being ....

Second, this conception of activity involves an extraordinary conception of causation according to which an agent, which is a substance and not an event, can nevertheless be the cause of an event.

A first point to be noted is that it appears that Taylor 1961/1992's central and perhaps only reason for deeming "*self* or *person*" to be a "rather strange metaphysical notion" is that it is "never applied elsewhere in nature." The SSP's response is that this lack of application elsewhere is in no way problematic or even surprising. According to the SSP, human beings differ from all other natural entities in a great variety of ways, so any adequate ontology must include factors pertaining only to them.[11] Being a self or person is one of those, and being an agent is another.

Of agency, Taylor 1961/1992 objects not only that it characterizes nothing in nature other than human beings, but also that it cannot be accounted for by the ontology the work presupposes. Just why it cannot is perhaps clarified by the following: "No one seems able, as we have noted, to describe deliberation without metaphors, and the

---

[11] Near its end, Taylor 1961/1999 acknowledges (83) the unique status of human beings: "the world is mysterious and ... we who try to understand it are even more so." If indeed human beings are more mysterious than the (non-human?) world, then adequate theories concerning human beings will have to contain (in the words of Taylor 1961/1999) notions that are never applied elsewhere in nature.

conception of a thing's being 'within one's power' or 'up to him' seems to defy analysis or definition altogether, if taken in the sense that the theory of agency appears to require."

It is not clear what Taylor 1961/1992 would require by way of analysis or definition, but it is important to note that children begin early on to converse about their powers, presumably most commonly by talking about what they can and can't do, and to understand situations in which they are told that something or other is up to them. As for the "metaphors" required to describe deliberation, a putative example (39) is talk of "trying to anticipate consequences of various possible courses of action," but nothing in this phrase is problematically metaphorical. Taylor 1961/1992 says of it in addition that "such descriptions do not convey to us what deliberation is unless we already know," but anyone capable of understanding such a description of course *does* already know what deliberation is, having experienced it repeatedly while acquiring the linguistic competence required for understanding the description. In addition, if human beings did *not* know what it means to try to anticipate consequences of various possible courses of action, it is wholly unclear why their languages would or even could develop so as to enable them to talk of such matters.

One final passage from Taylor 1961/1992 merits brief consideration; it reads (53), "Deliberation becomes, on [the libertarian] view, something that is not only possible but quite rational, for it does make sense to deliberate about activity that is truly my own and that depends in its outcome on me as its author, and not merely on something more or less esoteric that is supposed to be intimately associated with me, such as my thoughts, volitions, and choices."

Here again, problematic presuppositions are at work. What is esoteric about thoughts, volitions, and choices? It appears empirically to be the case that all natural languages enable their users to converse intelligibly about what they think, what they want, and choices they have made or are confronted with. At least often, children begin to use this language when they are quite young. The child who is told, "We have to go now, so if you don't decide which kind of ice cream you want, you won't be able to have any" is not, typically, baffled. Instead, the child understands the alternatives presented by the sentence, and often exercises the capacity—or, in Taylor 1961/1992's term, power—to make a choice. Talk of thoughts, volitions, and choices is thus *exoteric, not* esoteric. We often deliberate *when we have conflicting wants*; when we deliberate, we do so by *thinking*; and we often conclude deliberations by *choosing* (sometimes choosing to postpone deliberation). Theories *denying* that human beings have thoughts and volitions, and that they make choices, are the ones that qualify as esoteric.

6.3.1.2 Strawson

As indicated above (6.3), several works published by Galen Strawson between 1986 and (at least) 2011 present versions of a "Basic Argument" putatively establishing the truth of anti-libertarianism. One version of the argument is the following (2008: 319–20):

1   Interested in free action, we are particularly interested in actions that are performed for a reason (as opposed to 'reflex' actions or mindlessly habitual actions).

2   When one acts for a reason, what one does is a function of

how one is, mentally speaking. (It is also a function of one's height, one's strength, one's place and time, and so on. But the mental factors are crucial when moral responsibility is in question.)

3   So if one is to be truly responsible for how one acts, one must be truly responsible for how one is, mentally speaking—at least in certain respects.

4   But to be truly responsible for how one is, mentally speaking, in certain respects, one must have brought it about that one is the way one is, mentally speaking, in certain respects. And it is not merely that one must have caused oneself to be the way one is, mentally speaking. One must have consciously and explicitly chosen to be the way one is, mentally speaking, in certain respects, and one must have succeeded in bringing it about that one is that way.

5   But one cannot really be said to choose, in a conscious, reasoned, fashion, to be the way one is mentally speaking, in any respect at all, unless one already exists, mentally speaking, already equipped with some principles of choice, 'P1'—preferences, values, pro-attitudes, ideals—in the light of which one chooses how to be.

6   But then to be truly responsible, on account of having chosen to be the way one is, mentally speaking, in certain respects, one must be truly responsible for one's having the principles of choice P1 in the light of which one chose how to be.

7   But for this to be so one must have chosen P1, in a reasoned, conscious, intentional fashion.

8 But for this, that is, (7), to be so one must already have had some principles of choice P2 in the light of which one chose P1.

9 And so on. Here we are setting out on a regress that we cannot stop. True self-determination is impossible because it requires the actual completion of an infinite series of choices of principles of choice. [Footnote 2: That is, the infinite series must have a beginning and an end, which is impossible.]

10 So true moral responsibility is impossible, because it requires true self-determination, as noted in (3).

Strawson 2008 was written, it says, "in the hope that anyone who thinks that we can be truly or ultimately morally responsible for our actions will be prepared to say exactly what is wrong with the Basic Argument." According to the SSP, its central error—a fatal one—is its failure to clarify what is involved in choosing "in a reasonable, conscious, intentional fashion." Specifically, it fails to recognize the facts (1) that human beings confronted with choices to be made or acts to be done in light of reasons can and indeed often do have, among their "principles of choice" a "preference" for proceeding rationally, involving something like a "pro-attitude" toward the "value" truth; and (2) that human beings who choose to proceed rationally and succeed in doing so precisely thereby transcend the "principles of choice" that they *happen* to have acquired in the course of their previous experience in that they can examine and evaluate those principles, in part by comparing them with other principles of which they can become aware by thinking, conversing with others, and reading. Perhaps ironically but not wholly surprisingly, Strawson

2008 appears elsewhere to acknowledge that human beings can proceed rationally, in reporting (321) its author's belief that "it is the natural light, not fear"—and not any idiosyncratic preferences, values, pro-attitudes, or ideals—that has led all of his students not misled by "religious convictions" (321n. 3) to confirm the validity and soundness of the Basic Argument.

A closely related objection to the Basic Argument emerges from recognition that Strawson 2008 fails to take into consideration the fact that moral responsibility is only one of many forms of human responsibility. Of central importance is what may be termed intellectual responsibility. If indeed Strawson 2008 presents a theory—if it is not, for example, an elaborate joke or satire—then it is a work whose author, in presenting the completed work, accepts responsibility for presenting as true the thesis that ultimate moral responsibility, for human beings, is impossible. The author discharges this responsibility by presenting and defending the work's various versions of the Basic Argument. As should be clear given the discussion above of the restricted biologically programmed operator, Strawson 2008—like *every* work that presents a theory—*must* contain sentences governed ultimately by the theoretical operator "It is true that." Theoreticians who choose to assess such sentences (instead of investigating other subject matters) attempt, first, to determine whether or not they are indeed true, relying on procedures that involve deliberation and thus presuppose libertarianism.[12]

---

[12] A theoretician choosing instead the task of writing a biography of Galen Strawson would not, in the first instance, and perhaps not in any instance, be concerned with determining whether or not the conclusion of the Basic Argument is true. The biographer would be concerned instead with the truth of sentences such as "[It is true that] Galen Strawson first published a version of the Basic Argument in 1986."

Returning to the topic of moral responsibility: although Strawson 2008 asserts that it is "important to try to be precise about what sort of responsibility is under discussion," it fails to attain the requisite precision. To achieve what it presents as the requisite precision, it introduces "the story of heaven and hell": "As I understand it, true moral responsibility is responsibility of such a kind that, if we had it, then it *makes sense*, at least, to suppose that it could be just to punish some of us with (eternal) torment in hell and reward others with (eternal) bliss in heaven" (322). This sentence—on which the work does not elaborate—fails to make clear whether *all* who did not merit eternal reward would merit eternal torment, or whether instead there might be one or more other options (such as purgatory or reincarnation). Strawson 2008 suggests that such clarifications are unnecessary because the understanding of ultimate moral responsibility it articulates is widely held. Without providing any empirical support, the piece asserts that this is "the kind of moral of responsibility" (321) or "sort of moral responsibility" (322) that "many suppose" we have (321), that "has for a long time been central to the Western religious, moral, and cultural tradition" (321), that is "widely believed in" (322), "that many have supposed themselves to have, and that many do still suppose themselves to have" (322), "that we ordinarily suppose" (326), that is "the natural, strong understanding of the notion" (327), and that is "central to ordinary thought about moral responsibility and justice" (327). To support its denial that its sense of moral responsibility is exclusively Western, the article asserts the following:

> it is significant that anthropologists have suggested that most human societies can be classified either as 'guilt cultures' or as

'shame cultures.' It is true that neither of these two fundamental moral emotions necessarily presupposes a conception of oneself as truly morally responsible for what one has done. But the fact that both are widespread does at least suggest that a conception of moral responsibility similar to our own is a natural part of the human moral-conceptual repertoire. (321–2)

Strawson 2008 fails to note that "a conception of moral responsibility similar to our own" is a conception that is *different* from "our own"— or, more accurately, the article's own—to a greater or lesser degree.

6.3.2 Human freedom and the natural sciences

6.3.2.1 *Human freedom and the physical domain*

One objection often raised against libertarianism is that libertarian theories remain inadequate if they fail to include accounts of just how an event in the mental domain—for example, the event of *deciding* to raise a hand during a discussion—triggers an event in the physical domain—the movement of the hand. The SSP agrees that this is a theoretical issue open to investigation, but notes the current unavailability of any theoretical frameworks within which such investigation can take place. The SSP also notes the following: First, presumably all theories that recognize mental as well as physical domains acknowledge that there are cases in which physical events are involved in triggering mental events. As an example, the physical events of light rays striking retinas and of firings of neurons are involved in triggering mental events of visual awareness or of coming to know. Second, there are no currently available theoretical frameworks within which the issue of just how the physical events are involved in triggering the mental events can be investigated. The lack of such frameworks does not bring into question the thesis that there is such involvement.

This may be put less technically. Human beings cannot have visual experience, in the sense of seeing their surroundings, if their eyes are closed. Normally, the physical event of the raising of eyelids results in visual experience. *How* the transition from the physical to the experiential (or mental) takes place is not explained by any available theory. *That* it takes place reveals that its explanation is a topic open to theoretical investigation. At present, however, the link from the physical domain to the experiential (or mental) domain is mysterious, precisely because of the lack of theoretical explanations of it. But that it is mysterious is not a reason to deny that there is such a link or that developing theoretical frameworks within which it can be explained is a significant theoretical desideratum.

The same holds for the link between the experiential (or mental) domain and the physical domain. My deciding that now is the time for me to raise my hand during the discussion period following a lecture is generally linked to the raising of my hand—the mental event of deciding is linked to the physical event of hand-raising. *How* the transition from the mental to the physical takes place is not explained by any available theory. *That* it takes place reveals that its explanation is a topic open to theoretical investigation. At present, however, the link from the mental domain to the physical domain is mysterious, precisely because of the lack of theoretical explanations of it. But that it is mysterious is not a reason to deny that it exists or that developing theoretical frameworks within which it can be explained is a significant theoretical desideratum.

The theses that there are no currently available theories explaining physical-to-mental links or mental-to-physical links are, of course, empirical. Development and presentation of such theories would therefore lead to their alteration.

6.3.2.2 *Human freedom and evolution*

Human beings emerge during the process of evolution as beings that, under various circumstances, cannot avoid deliberating. Deliberation requires physical energy—deliberation is linked to events within the brain—and deliberation can have deleterious physical consequences, as when worry leads to insomnia or to distractedness while driving, in cases when accidents ensue. If, as according to currently widely accepted epiphenomenal theories, deliberation were not efficacious—if what human beings did resulted wholly from physical events, including prominently among them ones within the brain—then deliberation (and indeed consciousness) would be evolutionarily detrimental. If on the other hand, as according to the SSP, deliberation can be efficacious then it can be evolutionarily advantageous because it can enable human beings to make innovative responses when in novel situations. Hence, libertarianism conjoins with evolutionary theory more coherently and intelligibly than does determinism or anti-libertarianism.

Attempts made within non-libertarian frameworks to explain how deliberation could be advantageous cannot avoid relying on libertarian theses. An example reveals the pattern detectable elsewhere. The example is from (J. J. C.) Smart 2005, a response to the excellent Hodgson 2005, "A Plain Person's Free Will." The response contains the following passage:

It may well be that consciousness in the full sense is just awareness of awareness, coming to believe by inner sense about the brain processes that are the comings to believe about the external world (Smart, 2004, and Armstrong in Armstrong and Malcolm, [1984]). We approximate to mere awareness when we go on to 'automatic pilot' as Armstrong has put it …. The second order awareness would have evolutionary value because of its monitoring of first order awareness ….

Hodgson suggests that if consciousness was not necessary for … free choice then it would confer no selective advantage and indeed that if one were confronted by a crisis, for example the approach of a tiger, natural selection would not have made us waste our mental power on consciousness, whereas the opposite is the case: if a man eating tiger approaches a man he has heightened consciousness. I can agree about the heightened consciousness but draw a different conclusion: the more critical the situation the more important it may be to monitor one's awareness. (62)

Crucial here is Smart 2005's unexplained and unwarranted shift from second-order *awareness* to *monitoring*. If it is no shift—if there is no more to monitoring than there is to awareness—then the alleged evolutionary advantage disappears. If I were merely *aware* of how my automatic pilot was responding to the approach of the tiger, I might (I suppose) be pleased by my expertise or dismayed by my incompetence, but either would indeed involve a waste of brain power. If on the other hand I am to *monitor* the auto-pilot, in any sense that has potential evolutionary value, I must be in a position to *override* it—and that requires a capacity beyond that of mere awareness. Put somewhat differently: it appears that Smart 2005's "heightened awareness" is forced on me precisely when my auto-pilot fails. Of course, it could be argued that my auto-pilot has not failed, that it is simply confronted with a problem for which it requires time to compute the solution, but in that case, again, the awareness has no value—I will do whatever my auto-pilot dictates when the computation has been completed.

Within its theoretical framework, then, Smart 2005 faces a dilemma that it cannot escape: if its "monitoring" is no more than awareness, then it is evolutionarily detrimental. It has evolutionary value only if it involves the capacity to intervene, but its intervention would be, in Hodgson 2005's terms, "something else [that] *does* contribute to the determination of what actually happens"—the free choice, perhaps, to make the dangerous dive into the river far below rather than to embark on the almost certainly futile footrace (or to tremble in terror, etc.).

6.3.2.3 *Human freedom and neuroscience*

A number of similar experiments purporting to disprove human freedom manifestly fail to do so. Only the following example (Soon et al. 2008) need be considered here[13]:

> The subjects were asked to relax while fixating on the center of the screen where a stream of letters was presented. At some point, when they felt the urge to do so, they were to freely decide between one of two buttons, operated by the left and right index fingers, and press it immediately. In parallel, they should remember the letter presented when their motor decision was consciously made ....

---

[13] Similar experiments are reported in Libet et al. 1983, Libet et al. 1999, and Wegner 2002.

[M]ost of the intentions (88.6%) were reported to be consciously formed in 1,000 ms before the movement (…). (543–4)

Among the results was that the experimenters identified (544) "predictive neural information" that "will have preceded the conscious motor decision by up to 10 [seconds]." In other words, brain activity correlated with which button would be pushed occurred well before the subjects "decided" which button to push.

It is worth noting first that the actions of the experimental subjects are far from paradigmatically free ones, because nothing like deliberation is involved. Instead, the subjects were instructed to respond to their urges to act by "deciding." It is far from obvious that they could act in accordance with the instructions. They were to wait until they "felt an urge" to decide which button to press, and then to decide. What is unclear is whether any subject could determine which of the following is done: (1) (unconsciously) prepare to press a specific button, then (2) press the button on feeling the urge to do so; or (a) feel the urge to decide which button to press, then (b) make the decision.

If there is a plausible candidate for a subject's free decision anywhere on this horizon, it would be the decision to participate in the experiment—in the absence of which the subjects would never have felt the requisite urges.

6.4 Human freedom and systematic philosophy

It is well worth noting, in closing this chapter, that its course of argumentation could not develop without, and is tightly stabilized within, the systematic framework of the SSP. It relies on SSP theses concerning semantic determination, theoretical frameworks, and the necessity that theoreticians rely on such frameworks. The importance of this systematic consideration is also shown as follows. The sentence "Everything I do or say is wholly determined by physical processes in my brain," *considered in relative isolation*, appears to be intelligible and to be at least possibly true. The course of argumentation central to *TAPTOE*'s Chapter 6 shows that if any such sentence is considered *not* in relative isolation but *instead* as a constituent of a theory, and various key factors requisite to the development and presentation of theories are introduced, the sentence proves to be untenable precisely because it cannot be stably situated within any theory developed by any human being.

7

Beauty

τῶι μὲν θεῶι καλὰ πάντα

To God all beautiful

HERACLITUS[1]

Chapter 7 presents a sketch of a theory of or within what is generally termed aesthetics whose incorporation into the SSP, in place of the aesthetic theory sketched in *SB*'s section 4.3 (The Aesthetic World), increases—according to *TAPTOE*—the SSP's intelligibility and coherence. The chief reason for the increased intelligibility and coherence is that whereas *SB* draws its data primarily from works by Aquinas and Kant, *TAPTOE* identifies, as a far richer source of data, Kovach 1974, *Philosophy of Beauty*, a truly excellent book that has been almost universally ignored.[2]

---

[1] Hermann Diels, *Die Fragmente der Vorsokratiker. Griechisch und Deutsch.* 12th unchanged edition, ed. Walther Kranz. Dublin/Zürich: Weidmann, 1996. Volume 1, fragment 102 (p. 173).

[2] Also widely ignored are the many invaluable historical works of Wladyslaw Tatarkiewicz, central among them *A History of Six Ideas* and three-volume *History of Aesthetics*. Kovach 1974 exhibits historical knowledge comparable to that evident in the works of Tatarkiewicz, although providing less detail, but Kovach 1974 also presents a systematic theory embedded within a generally Aristotelian-Aquinian framework.

As indicated at various points above, the focus of Chapter 7 is beauty. In treating beauty, *TAPTOE* confronts a complex terminological issue that results from a series of historical accidents. The first such accident is that, although beauty has been treated by philosophers since before the time of Socrates, inquiry focusing on beauty was not identified by name until the eighteenth century, when Alexander Baumgarten termed it aesthetics. The second important historical accident is that "aesthetics" is, etymologically, a far from optimal designation for this area of inquiry. The word is rooted in the Greek word meaning (most often) sense perception; it therefore suggests on the one hand that aesthetics should be the study of sense perception, and on the other that—if aesthetics studies beauty rather than sense perception—beauty is primarily, and perhaps exclusively, perceived by the senses. Because the first of these suggestions is simply misleading and the second at best questionable, "aesthetics" is far from optimal as a designation for inquiry into beauty. As emphasized by Kovach 1974 (9), an incomparably better term is callology, "which means exactly and literally 'the science of beauty.'" For this reason, *TAPTOE* uses "callology," "callological," etc., rather than "aesthetic," "aesthetics," etc. Consequently, callological delight is the kind of delight that is a subject matter for callology, the science of beauty; callological experience is the kind of experience that is a subject matter for callology.

Individual subsections (7.1–10) are devoted, respectively, to the following central theses of this subtheory:

C1: There are times when human beings are delighted by merely becoming aware of specific factings; the delight then experienced is callological delight.

C2: Callological delight can be and often is accompanied by other emotions; especially when experiencing complex works of art, human beings can (for example) be both delighted and amused (as by comedies), or both delighted and depressed (as by some tragedies).

C3: Every facting that has the capacity to callologically delight any human being is beautiful; its being beautiful does not require that this capacity be activated.

C4: Callological experience—the experience of callological delight—is distinct from both everyday and scientific callological evaluation in that there can be such delight unaccompanied by such evaluation, and such evaluation unaccompanied by such delight.

C5: Every facting save God is beautiful to the degree that it is an integral unity of proportionate constituents; if God has no constituents, then God's beauty consists in God's being an integral unity.

C6: All factings are beautiful, but there are great differences in their degrees of beauty.

C7: Factings whose degrees of beauty are low are conveniently termed ugly, but ugliness has no ontological status.

C8: That factings that on some occasions callologically delight some human beings do not on all occasions delight all human beings is best explained by differences among those human beings, including differences between any human being on one occasion and that human being on other occasions.

7.1 Callological delight

C1: There are times when human beings are delighted by merely becoming aware of specific factings; the delight then experienced is callological delight.[3]

Thesis C1, according to *TAPTOE*, is central to the best explanations of a vast array of human experiences. Although much work in recent and contemporary aesthetics focuses on the domain of fine art, the experiences in which callological delight are most clearly evident at least include ones of natural phenomena (factings): sunsets, rainbows, flowers, mountains, and so forth. All that thesis C1 requires, in order to be true, is that sometimes, some human beings, coming to know any phenomena at all, are delighted by that knowledge, and not by any actual or anticipated benefit from the phenomena or from the knowledge.

An example not only clarifies but stabilizes C1: once, driving through the Scottish highlands with his family, *TAPTOE*'s author saw, through the car's windshield, a particularly striking rainbow. He pulled off the road—as had several other drivers—and he, his wife, and his two children stared at the rainbow. He—and, according to their testimony, the members of his family—were, in *TAPTOE*'s terms, callologically delighted by it. This single example stabilizes C1 because C1 is quite modest. Any theory rejecting it would have to hold that no human being, ever, has been or could be delighted

[3] A subtheory of human emotions, including delight—a theory of affectivity—would be included in more complete concretizations of the SSP's theories concerning human beings within the universe (*SB*: The Human World [section 4.2]).

by merely coming to know, or becoming aware of, any specific phenomenon: not by any rainbow, any sunset, any painting, any film, any musical performance—not by anything at all.

7.2 Complex callological delight

C2: Callological delight can be and often is accompanied by other emotions; especially when experiencing complex works of art, human beings can (for example) be both delighted and amused (as by comedies), or both delighted and depressed (as by some tragedies).

As indicated in 7.1, callological delight is included in *TAPTOE* because it is central to the best explanations of why human beings choose to extend or to seek out experiences for reasons other than that they take those experiences to be beneficial or useful to them,[4] or morally required of them. The technical use of "delight" in *TAPTOE*'s term "callological delight" is—not surprisingly—not found, *per se*, in ordinary English. Readers of depressing novels, like many by Thomas Hardy, or viewers of disturbing films, like many directed by Ingmar Bergmann, might well be, as a matter of empirical fact, unlikely to say that they had been delighted by reading the novels

---

[4]Reverting to the example above: *TAPTOE*'s author's experience of the rainbow in Scotland later proved useful to him by providing him with an example usable in various philosophy classes and in *TAPTOE*. Possibly, that experience was also psychologically beneficial to him. It remains the case, however, that his stopping to stare at the rainbow is best explained by his callological delight in his knowledge of it, and not by any considerations of utility or benefit.

or viewing the films. But at least some such readers or viewers who were absorbed in the reading or viewing, and who continued to read or view despite being depressed or disturbed, were, according to *TAPTOE*, callologically delighted by the readings or viewings: their callological delight explains their continuing to read or view. Again, this need not always be the case for thesis C2 to be true—some might continue to read or view for other reasons, for example to satisfy course requirements. For thesis C2 to be true, it need only *sometimes* be the case.

Complex callological delight is clarified by examples. What if, as a film ends, a viewer honestly exclaims, "That was terrifying! It was great!"? In most circumstances, of course, it is not great to be terrified. But it can be great to be terrified by a film (or a play or a novel, etc.). *TAPTOE* explains this phenomenon by saying that the viewer was both delighted and terrified. Had the viewer just been terrified—had they not also been delighted—then their honest reaction would have been something like "That was terrifying! I hated it!". Their watching it to its end would then be explained by something other than callological delight; perhaps they hoped that as it continued it would begin to delight them, or perhaps they were with friends they did not want to abandon.

An additional distinction further clarifies callological delight. "That was terrifying! It was great!" could also be uttered, honestly, by a person who had just taken a roller-coaster ride. In this case, too, the person would have been both delighted and terrified, but the delight would not have been callological delight because what caused the terror would have been a sense of *personal* rather than *vicarious* danger. The viewer terrified by the film is terrified by the danger to or harm done to one or more characters in the film—and such terror can contribute to callological delight.

7.3 Callological delight and beauty

C3: Every facting that has the capacity to callologically delight any human being is beautiful; its being beautiful does not require that this capacity be activated.

In terms relied on in various traditional frameworks, the SSP's theory of beauty is an objectivism rather than a subjectivism. More technically, its theory is one according to which there are factings that, utterly independently of human beings, include among their constituents members of the family IT's-BEING-BEAUTIFUL.

Consideration of the relative merits of objectivisms and subjectivisms about beauty is aided by the introduction of what Kovach 1974 terms the positive aesthetic fact. The positive aesthetic (or: callological) fact is a version of *TAPTOE*'s thesis C1; one of Kovach 1974's formulations (55) is "Occasionally, some people, while beholding certain objects, experience delight." The SSP's version of this fact—the SSP's facting—qualifies the delight as callological delight, and speaks not of objects, but instead of factings that exist independently of their being beheld by any human being (henceforth: i-factings).[5]

---

[5] It is possible for people to be callologically delighted by wholly intramental factings; clear cases would include those of artists who clearly imagined works before producing them, and were callologically delighted by what they imagined; see Kovach 1974, 60.

The SSP's explanation of the positive callological fact is straightforward: people experience callological delight on merely coming to know specific i-factings because those i-factings are beautiful. What is the subjectivist alternative? In the case of the example introduced above in 7.1, the subjectivist cannot say that what explains *TAPTOE's* author's stopping to stare at the rainbow is his becoming aware of—his coming to know—the rainbow's beauty. The subjectivist might suggest that because what delighted the author was his knowledge, it was the knowledge that was beautiful. But what made his knowledge the specific knowledge that it was was precisely its being knowledge of the rainbow.

If the subjectivist who has experienced callological delight does not identify their knowledge as beautiful, then the subjectivist must hold that their delight is inexplicable—that they just happen to be delighted, and that the rainbow had nothing to do with it. But if that is the case, the delight is not callological delight, because it is unrelated to any instance of merely coming to know. And although there may well be experiences in which human beings simply find that they are delighted, and are unable to say why, that is not the case with callological delight; the subject who is callologically delighted upon seeing a rainbow knows that the rainbow is the source of their delight.[6]

That the rainbow callologically delights anyone establishes that it has the *capacity* to callologically delight; had it lacked that capacity, the callological delight would have been impossible. But what, then, of phenomena that callologically delighted no human beings because they were experienced by no human beings—what, for example, of

---

[6] To be sure, they might say that what delighted them was the rainbow rather than their coming to know the rainbow, but they would presumably acknowledge that had they not come to know the rainbow, they would not have been callologically delighted.

phenomena such as flowers that bloomed during the time of the dinosaurs? According to *TAPTOE*, there were, during that time, beautiful flowers. Just as a food's capacity to nourish a human being is activated only if the food is consumed by the human being, the beautiful flower's capacity to callologically delight—its beauty—is activated only if it callologically delights a human being. Beauty, according to *TAPTOE*, is this capacity, *not* its activation, and capacities such as these are full-fledged ontological constituents of factings.

7.4 Callological delight and callological evaluation

C4: Callological experience—the experience of callological delight—is distinct from both everyday and scientific callological evaluation in that there can be such delight unaccompanied by such evaluation, and such evaluation unaccompanied by such delight.

Failure to recognize this distinction is a cause of enormous confusion in the philosophical literature. One way to reveal the distinction is by noting that infants normally begin to have callological experiences long before they are able to articulate callological or aesthetic evaluations. Infants' delight in being read stories or nursery rhymes, in looking at picture books, in hearing music, and so forth is often, according to *TAPTOE*, callological delight. Callological or aesthetic evaluation, on the other hand, is a *theoretical* engagement that requires one or another theoretical framework that includes vocabulary items not intelligible to young infants.

The distinction is clarified by the following example: Bob has come to view a film in the hope of callologically delighting in it, whereas Sarah has come because she agreed to write a review to be posted by the following morning. The greater the degree to which Bob's hope is realized, the more fully absorbed in the film he will be, and the less involved in assessing its callological or aesthetic merits. If the absorption is extreme, there is no such involvement whatsoever. At the opposite extreme, two things can be true of Sarah. First, it can be the case that if she'd come to see the film without having agreed to review it, she would have been callologically delighted by it. Second, it can be the case that, having agreed to review it, she fully concentrates on taking notes that will aid her in writing the review, and consequently experiences no callological delight whatsoever.

A case more extreme even than that of Sarah is that of Iris. Improbably but possibly, Iris, although deaf, is a music scholar specializing in symphonies. Having either developed or accepted a theoretical framework for ranking symphonies as more or less beautiful, and having learned to read music, Iris writes first-rate comparative evaluations of symphonies despite her inability to be callologically delighted by performances of them.

Not all cases, of course, are so extreme. Experiencing callological delight of lesser intensity, people can—according to *TAPTOE*—utter callological or aesthetic evaluations of them while the delight is ongoing.[7] In addition, the greater the sophistication of (say) a film viewer, the better (as a rule) will that viewer be able to provide a

---

[7] Kovach 1974 (313) recognizes but does not explicitly accept the thesis that this can happen.

sophisticated evaluation just after having been intensely callologically delighted by a film. But that the extremes of callological delight in the absence of callological evaluation and callological evaluation in the absence of callological delight *are* extremes does not diminish their significance: the distinction is centrally important.

7.5 All factings are beautiful

C5: Every facting save God is beautiful to the degree that it is an integral unity of proportionate constituents; if God has no constituents, then God's beauty consists in God's being an integral unity.

Leaving aside at this point the exceptional cases of simple factings (if there are any) and God, every other facting is complex and thus has constituents. Every complex facting, as having constituents, necessarily includes as constituents the following three relations: the relation of the facting to its constituents, the relation of the constituents to one another, and the relation of the constituents to the facting. According to *TAPTOE*—again reconfiguring data whose source is Kovach 1974 (see 184–215)—the relation of facting to constituents is that of unifying or unification: the facting unifies its constituents. The relation of constituents to one another is proportionality; they are, necessarily, sufficiently proportionate to one another to enable the facting to be the facting that it is. The relation of constituents to facting is integrity: all of the constituents required by the facting, to be the facting that it is, must be included among its constituents.

An example, relying on a minimally articulated framework for a theory of visual beauty situated within the SSP's framework, clarifies. A given human body, as visually beautiful,[8] unifies or is the unity of arms, legs, head, and so forth. It can exist, as the body of a human being, only if there are no fatal disproportionalities among its constituents, and only if it has all the constituents that are required for its continuing to live, and thus are integral to it. After a human being dies, there is often a corpse, and it will be a more or less beautiful corpse, but not a more or less beautiful human body. The visual beauty of a given human body, as a human body, depends on the degrees (1) to which its visible constituents are proportionate to one another, (2) to which it has all of the visible constituents that human bodies normally have, and (3) to which those constituents are intuitively intelligible as a unity.

To clarify factor (3): a novelist might conclude that their work had all the constituents (characters, scenes, conversations, and so forth) that were integral to it—that it required—and none that were superfluous, and that those constituents were proportionate to one another (no scene too long or short, no character given too much or too little attention, and so forth), but that the work was not sufficiently unified—that it did not, in colloquial terms, hang together. The novelist might, in principle, solve the problem by putting the

---

[8] "As visually beautiful" is importantly distinct from "as sexually attractive"; the viewer who is sexually attracted may or may not be callologically delighted, to some degree, but the greater the sexual attraction, the less the aesthetic delight, because the more intense the callological delight, the more satisfied is the viewer with beholding the source of the delight, and the less engaged in being attracted to it. The variety of uses of "beauty," "beautiful," etc., in ordinary English is of no relevance to the SSP, within which these are technical terms with specified meanings.

constituents into a different order. One possible case: a deed that had appeared unmotivated ceases to appear so if a conversation is moved so as to precede the deed. To be sure, so pure a case of failure of unity in conjunction with success of proportionality and integrity presumably rarely if ever takes place. But the point should be clear. *TAPTOE* explains the activity of the artist at work to increase the beauty (in TAPTOE's sense) of a given piece[9] as consisting of work to maximize its integrity—by including in the work all the constituents it needs, and excluding from it any that it does not—proportionality—by correcting imbalances among the (integral) constituents—and unity—by arranging the integral and proportionate constituents into an intuitively intelligible unity. When the artist, perhaps after consulting selected readers, sees no way to improve integrity, proportionality, or unity, nothing more is to be done.

"Intuitively intelligible," used twice in preceding paragraphs, requires clarification. Following Kovach 1974, *TAPTOE* distinguishes intuitive intelligibility from discursive intelligibility. Intelligibility is discursive when it requires and therefore results (in part) from explanation. The beauty of a symphony, for example, may be made discursively intelligible by a scientific evaluation of it. Having read the evaluation, one who had never heard the symphony might come to accept as true the thesis that the symphony is exceptionally beautiful, and might be able to provide an excellent explanation of how it is, given the criteria provided by the evaluatory framework, that it

---

[9]To be sure, not all who call themselves or are called by others "artists" work always or exclusively to produce works that are beautiful. "Artist," in ordinary English, is quite vague (as is, of course, "beauty"). These vaguenesses are irrelevant to the SSP.

qualifies as exceptionally beautiful. But that would not guarantee that, hearing the symphony, that person would find the piece to be intuitively intelligible as an integral unity of proportionate constituents, and hence be callologically delighted. As suggested above, that person could even be deaf.

From the theses (1) that every complex facting is an integral unity of proportionate constituents and (2) that to be an integral unity of proportionate constituents is to be beautiful, it follows that (3; see C5) every complex facting is beautiful. Given in addition the theses (4 = C3) that to be beautiful is to have the capacity to callologically delight human beings and (5) that any conjunction of factings is a facting (see *SB*, 208), it also follows (6) that any collection whatsoever of factings is beautiful, and therefore has the capacity to delight human beings. To be sure, for the overwhelming majority of factings, and even the overwhelming majority of factings that human beings come to know, this capacity will presumably remain unactivated. But whereas it might appear ontologically extravagant to attribute to all factings this capacity that, in most, will remain unactivated, the rejection of this thesis is more extreme, because the rejection involves some version of the thesis that there is at least one facting such that that facting could not possibly callologically delight any human being who, in any circumstances whatsoever, came to know it. *TAPTOE* recognizes no way in which this thesis could be stabilized, particularly given that even factings whose degrees of beauty are quite low can, if incorporated into works of art, contribute to experiences of callological delight.

Two questions remain to be addressed in this subsection: (1) are there simple physical factings? And (2) is God simple? First, to (1):

simple physical factings, if there are any (and whether or not there are is a question to be addressed by physicists), would, according to SB (214), be minimally structured as self-identical. The constituents of the simple facting, as so structured, would be itself and its relation of identity to itself. The simple facting would be the unity of these two integral constituents, and the two could not be disproportionate to each other. The simple physical facting would thereby qualify as beautiful. Moreover, human beings could come to know such factings as they were articulated in theories; the appearance of such factings, within the theories, could callologically delight human beings who came to understand those theories.

As for (2): first, given the principle of rank within being (8.3.6.2, below), God is beautiful. The question is, does God have constituents, or is God simple? *TAPTOE* leaves this question open. If according to the *SSP*'s theory of God, when further developed, God has constituents, then God's beauty will consist in God's being an integral unity of proportionate constituents. If instead, according to that theory, God has no constituents—if, in general accordance with (among others) the theology of Aquinas, God is simple—then God's beauty will consist in God's being an integral unity without proportionate constituents: a unity because one, and integral because lacking nothing God requires in order to be God (see Kovach 1974, 212–214).

A final remark is in order. In Chapter IX, which presents, explains, and defends its essential definition of beauty, Kovach 1974 strongly distinguishes between material and immaterial beings, explicitly identifying (208), as candidate immaterial beings and corresponding beauties, "the human act or virtue (moral beauty), spiritual substances, including the human soul (spiritual beauty), and God (divine beauty)," and asserting (211) that "No immaterial being is directly knowable." This passage is symptomatic of an uncharacteristic defect in the argumentation of Kovach 1974, that is, its only sporadic recognition of the fact that the beauty of works of literature is not material beauty. *TAPTOE*, in full agreement with *SB* on this issue, remedies the defect by according full-fledged ontological status to this directly knowable (experienceable) form of immaterial beauty. It is directly knowable (in Kovach's sense) because it is experienced, most often when one reads—it does not emerge only as the conclusion of an argument.

7.6 Degrees of beauty

C6: All factings are beautiful, but there are great differences in their degrees of beauty.

As indicated above in various contexts, determining degrees of beauty is a matter of theoretical (and, in some cases, scientific) evaluation, including the theoretical evaluation made (perhaps generally implicitly) by the artist at work. An oversized nose might be disproportionate in a portrait but proportionate in a caricature. A lengthy digression might be disproportionate in a detective novel but proportionate in a comedy. In determining degrees of beauty, any evaluational theory embedded within the SSP's theoretical framework will consider, centrally, the factors of unity, integrity, and proportionality.

7.7 Ugliness

C7: Factings whose degrees of beauty are low are conveniently termed ugly, but ugliness has no ontological status.

The word "ugliness" and its conjugates enrich the vocabulary of *TAPTOE*'s callological theory, but *TAPTOE*'s ontology does not include any instances of IT's BEING-UGLY that would exclude, from factings within which they were constituents, instances of IT's BEING-BEAUTIFUL. To the contrary, sentences including "ugly" or any of its conjugates express propositionings of the likes of *It's being-beautiful-to-a-low-degree*. The semantic status of ugliness is, then, similar to that of shortness, as clarifying height, in the most common everyday frameworks. In such frameworks one can intelligibly ask of any human being, "How tall is she?". One cannot intelligibly ask, "How short is she?" except in cases where the person in question has previously been identified as short. If the answer to "How tall is she?" is "four feet," then the person in question is short if she is an adult, but not if she is a two-year-old.

Hence, in any evaluatory callological theory situated within the broader theoretical framework of the SSP, art works or aspects of art works could be criticized for being ugly, and aspects of art works that in isolation from them would qualify as ugly could be identified as contributing to the beauty of the works in which they were situated.

Worth noting as well is that phenomena commonly classified as ugly, even as repulsive, may also be instances of what is illuminatingly termed difficult beauty. Kovach 1974 includes (123) the following example, from Cory 1947 (180–81):

If I look at a dead, rotting body as a human body—which it is not—I do not find it beautiful. But I learned a long time ago, in the laboratories of the Johns Hopkins University, to discern in the chemical changes of physiological deterioration, in the wonderful purifying work of the saprophytic bacteria, the emergence of a number of simple but unimpeachably beautiful entities.

7.8 Callological disagreement

C8: That factings that on some occasions callologically delight some human beings do not on all occasions delight all human beings is best explained by differences among those human beings, including differences between any human being on one occasion and that human being on other occasions.

That there is widespread callological disagreement among human beings appears to be the most important reason given in support of subjectivisms about beauty. *TAPTOE* of course acknowledges the existence of such disagreement, but contends that it is better explained by its objectivism than by any subjectivism.

"That was beautiful (or great, terrific, etc.)!", uttered by S1 as an everyday evaluation more or less immediately following an experience of callological delight, can be understood as expressing the proposition *That callologically delighted me*. So understood, this sentence is wholly consistent with S2's "That was horrible (or lousy, tedious, boring, etc.)!", uttered following S2's experience of the same phenomenon, if S2's utterance is understood as expressing the proposition *That failed miserably to callologically delight me.* S1's delight is explained by the activation of the phenomenon's capacity to callologically delight—hence, the phenomenon's beauty—*and* the activation of S1's capacity to be callologically delighted by beautiful phenomena. Explaining S2's lack of delight does not require denying that the phenomenon is beautiful; what must be explained is why, when S2 engaged with the phenomenon, S2's capacity for being callologically delighted was not activated.

Kovach 1974 (101–36) presents 36 reasons why phenomena that callologically delight some human beings, thereby revealing themselves as beautiful, fail to callologically delight other human beings. Some are simple; for example, blind people cannot be callologically delighted by visually beautiful phenomena, deaf people cannot be callologically delighted by the sounds of complex harmonies, and those who cannot understand a given language cannot be callologically delighted by the stories told in works of literature written in it. Some other reasons for callological disagreement are more complicated but nevertheless easily explicable. Because being callologically delighted by complex art works often requires extensive exposure and education, those lacking such exposure and education will wholly predictably fail to appreciate the beauty of such works.

Some disagreements arise of course not from differing experiences but from differing evaluations. Such disagreements are on the theoretical level, and are explained either by evaluators' relying on different theoretical frameworks, or by their presenting different concretizations of a shared framework. Such evaluations themselves, as theoretical, can be assessed comparatively.

8

Being

According to the Eleatic Visitor in Plato's *Sophist* (246a5), being [οὐσία] was of sufficient philosophical importance to his predecessors to have instigated "something like a battle of gods and giants among them." Shortly thereafter, being *qua* being [τὸ ὂν ᾗ ὄν] was identified in Aristotle's *Metaphysics* (1003a21) as the issue at the heart of first philosophy. Nevertheless, there are central issues concerning being that are not recognized by any Greek philosopher, indeed not identified until the thirteenth century, in some works by Thomas Aquinas. As explained more fully below, after Aquinas, these issues are recognized only quite sporadically. They are, however, a focus of the SSP, wherein their importance is indicated by the inclusion of the word "being" in the titles of the books *Structure and Being* and *Being and God*. This chapter sketches a theory of being that aims to improve on the theories of being sketched in those books by relying on a more refined language of being.

8.1 Articulating being

One centrally important reason for lack of sufficient clarity in philosophical treatments of being is that at least most of the languages
philosophers have relied on throughout the history of philosophy,
emphatically including English, articulate being in a variety of ways.
That they do so adds needless and often misleading complications to
this articulation. A first source of complications in ordinary English is
the vocabulary available for the articulation of being; a second source is
the structures of the sentences it provides for articulating being. Each
of the following two subsections first identifies specific problems with
ordinary-English ways of articulating being, and then introduces refine-
ments to the SSP's language that enables it to avoid these problems.

8.1.1 Refinements of vocabulary

Three peculiarities of the words used by ordinary English to articulate being are of particular importance as far as philosophical
articulations of being are concerned. The first peculiarity is that the
word "being" has (most relevantly) the following distinct senses: (1) a
nominal sense, in which "being" is roughly synonymous with "entity,"
and (2) a verbal sense, in which "being" is roughly synonymous
with "existence," in the sense articulated in the *OED* as "the fact of
belonging to the universe of things material or immaterial." Because
the two senses are available, one can say both "To be is to be a being"
and "To be is to be being." Philosophical uses of the word "being" that
do not clearly distinguish these senses, or that do not make clear, in
all relevant cases, which sense is intended, require clarification.

The second important peculiarity of words used in ordinary English to articulate being is that, because the word "is" is so often used as copula (or, on an alternative interpretation, as a component of predicates, as in "is red" or "is human"), such sentences as "Fred is" can appear to be incomplete; hearing the sentence "Fred is," one might well wonder, "Fred is *what*?". Relatedly, the question "Does God exist?" is more readily intelligible than is the question, "Is God?". Presumably in part because sentences ending with "is" so easily appear incomplete, what may be called the existential use of "is"[1] is most commonly accompanied by "there," in the phrase "there is."[2] In this phrase (as in the phrase "there are"), the "there" does not perform its usual locative role; it instead signals that the "is" (or "are") is existential rather than copulative (or predicative). That English can express the existential sense of being by "is," by "exists," and by "there is," with the first of these being the most problematic, introduces avoidable confusion.

The third important peculiarity in ordinary-English words used to articulate being is that several conjugated forms of the verb "to be" have roots different both from that of the infinitive and from those of one another; these include "am," "is," and "are." Consequently,

---

[1] As explained in 8.3.4, in the language of the SSP, the domain of existence is a subdomain of that of being (which is comprehensive); hence, in only some sentences of the form "S is" can the "is" be replaced by "exists" without altering the truth value, whereas in all sentences of the form "S exists," the "exists" can be replaced by "is" without altering the truth value. Nevertheless, for the sake of preliminary clarification, this section characterizes the use of "is" in any sentence of the form "S is" or "There is such-and-such" as an existential use of "is," to distinguish this from the copulative and predicative uses of "is."

[2] Compare French *il y a*, German *es gibt*, Spanish *hay*, and Italian *c'è*. It is interesting that French and Italian, like English, use phrases including words that are usually locatives, and that German and Spanish use verbs other than forms of their counterparts to "to be" (*Sein*, for German, *ser* and *estár*, for Spanish). Because of these features, none of these expressions directly articulates being.

although any sentence using any one of these words at least co-artic-
ulates being, the words themselves do not make that fully explicit.

One way to improve talk about being, using English, is to introduce
a capitalized version of the word (as *Being and God* does), and to
explicitly link that version to the existential sense of "being." That,
however, avoids only the first of the three peculiarities just identified.[3] *TAPTOE* therefore proceeds differently. First, instead of using
the word "being" in a nominal sense, in which it would be roughly
synonymous with the word "entity," it introduces for that sense the
technical term "be-er," a word comparable to such ordinary-language
terms as "runner," "swimmer," "writer," and "philosopher"; important
to emphasize is that just as running is not a runner, being is not a
be-er. Second, *TAPTOE* often uses "be" when ordinary English would
require "am," "is," or "are"—that is, as the sole form of its verb "to be"
in the simple present, and as a component of present-continuous
verbs. Whether or not the sentence "We be jammin'" is of use in
Jamaican English, it is intelligible, as are (for example) "I be talking,"
"You be listening," and "We be philosophizing." In the technical
language of *TAPTOE*, there be human be-ers; human be-ers be the
be-ers that be human. Their mode of being be being human.[4]

Grammatically, *TAPTOE*'s variants of parts of the verb "to be"
make that verb much more regular than it is in ordinary English.[5]
Philosophically, they enable the book to directly and explicitly

---

[3] It can also introduce new problems, chiefly because capitalization is standard, in English,
only for proper nouns, and "Being," at least in *BG*, is not primarily nominal.

[4] To decrease awkwardness, *TAPTOE* occasionally speaks of human beings, although
"human be-ers" would be more accurate.

[5] It remains irregular in not adding "s" to "be" in third-person singular uses.

articulate being and its ubiquity, and thereby, it is hoped, to present a more powerful obstacle than does ordinary English to the tendency to what is called in various of Heidegger's works forgetfulness or oblivion of being. In other words: these changes are meant to make it harder for us to fail to notice the ubiquity of being—to notice that whenever we are speaking or thinking, we are speaking or thinking of being.

8.1.2 A refinement of semantically significant sentence-structures

Drawing on several works by Etienne Gilson, 8.1.2 shows why the vocabulary introduced in 8.1.1 can make possible the direct and explicit articulation of being that is the strongest obstacle to the oblivion of being only if it is accompanied by a refinement of semantically significant sentence-structures. A first step is taken with clarification of the ubiquity of being as articulable in theories.

Theories are articulated as collections of indicative sentences and, as Gilson 1952 (197) points out (speaking of affirmations rather than, explicitly, of indicative sentences),

> the principle function of the verb is to affirm, and since affirmation remains the same whatever may happen to be affirmed, a single verb should suffice for all affirmations. In point of fact, there is such a verb, and it is "to be." If only spoken usage allowed it, we would never use any other one ... Not *I live*, or *I sit*, but *I am living*, *I am sitting* and likewise in all other cases.

If "am living" and "am sitting" are understood as present-continuous verbs rather than as including copulative uses of "am," then of course they are not forms of the verb "to be," but even then, they include forms of that verb, and therefore co-articulate being. Moreover, additional distinctions are necessary, for example between the likes of "She be running" and "She be a runner" or, more expansively, "She be a be-er who also (more specifically) be running (right now)" and "She be a be-er who also (more specifically) be a runner (even if not running right now)."

A consequence of the possibility of such reformulations is that every theoretical sentence can be made to co-articulate being. Yet, for reasons given in Gilson 1948 (284–5), co-articulation of being has not sufficed, historically, to counter the oblivion of being. One reason for this is that the sentences considered in that text, like most sentences in English and in most other languages that have been used by philosophers, include semantically significant grammatical subjects.

The relevant passage from Gilson 1948 (284–5) merits detailed commentary, but brief remarks suffice for present purposes.[6] According to that text (285)—altered to incorporate *TAPTOE*'s language of being—being is most directly articulated in sentences of the form, "S [a semantically significant subject] be"; any such sentence articulates "the composition of the subject with its act of being, it unites them in thought as they are already united in reality."[7]

---

[6] Detailed commentary would show that what the text says about what it terms judgments of attribution and judgments of existence is not fully coherent; the remarks in the main text take some liberties with the text in order to achieve coherence.

[7] To say that being, as "the act of being," enters into "composition" with something else—"the subject," in the passage to which this note is appended, or "the essence," in the passage quoted just below in the main text—is to articulate being as non-comprehensive, and thus to fail recognize its ubiquity. The focus in this section is on semantic problems that would remain even if that failure was avoided.

Yet although any such sentence unites them, the human intellect, the text tells us (284), tends to focus on the subject—the be-er—and thereby to neglect the "act of being." In any such sentence, being is articulated only "as included in the [be-er]," and that it is only so articulated

> is often serious, to the point of sometimes being catastrophic, because, as history has made us see, the spontaneous conceptualism of ordinary thought tends constantly to reinforce the essence of the [be-er] to the detriment of its act of [being]. Let us also add that this fact is easily explained because the [be-er] has more than its [being],[8] that is, it has its concept, which is the proper prey of reasoning reason [*raison raisonnante*]; it always seeks definitions.

Gilson 1948 recognizes, as the only sentence-forms that articulate being, "S is p" and "S is." As discussed above in various contexts, the SSP links its semantics and ontology not to sentence-forms including semantically significant subject-terms, but instead to sentences of the form "It's such-and-suching." This makes it easy to explicitly and exclusively articulate being *itself, not* being as included in any be-er. This is done by the sentence "It's being" (or "It be being"), whose only semantically significant term is its present-continuous verb.[9] The decisive contributions this formulation makes to the SSP's theory of being are explained in greater detail in what follows, but one that

---

[8] Because of the ubiquity of being, no be-er can have "more than" its being—anything "more" that it could have would have to *be*. Whatever is truly said of any be-er beyond that it be is not something other than its being, but instead a specification of its being. This is further clarified in what follows.

[9] The "It" in such sentences is considered in 8.3.1.

links to Gilson 1948 is appropriately included here. According to that text (248), if a sentence of the form "S is" is understood as articulating being, it says "not that the subject is itself, which is always true of everything, but [instead] that it is, which is not true, and moreover not always, except for some." As more fully explained in what follows, the SSP's sentence "It be being" is always true; that it is is a first indication of the primacy of being.

8.2 Theories of being and theories of be-ers

Most theories, throughout the history of philosophy, that theoretical frameworks relying on ordinary English would classify as theories of *being* are, in *TAPTOE's* language, theories of *be-ers*. Moreover, in this terminology (and, more broadly, in that of the SSP), theories of be-ers are ontologies. Theories of be-ers are concisely summarized by sentences of the form "To be a be-er is to be *x*," with *x* replaced by one or more nouns, with appropriate article(s). Most ontologies, both historically and at present, hold that to be a be-er is to be either a thing (or object or substance), or an attribute of a thing (a property or, in some variants, a relation). The SSP's ontology holds instead, as discussed above in various contexts, that to be a be-er is to be a fact (or, in *TAPTOE's* technical term, a facting).

In what follows, clarity is served by speaking of frameworks for theories of be-ers that including thing- or substance-ontologies as whatness-frameworks, because at least the most prominent members of that family of frameworks include identifiable versions of the thesis of the primacy of whatness, that is, the thesis that every be-er is, primarily, its whatness.[10] In Aristotelian frameworks, the problem of being is not recognized, so the primacy of whatness is the primacy of substance over at least accidental attributes: according to such frameworks, Alan White is, primarily, either a human being (essence) or the specific human being that he is (individual), but he must be that whatness in order to be, at some specific time, sitting rather than standing.

Far later than Aristotle, Thomas Aquinas takes an important step in recognizing, at least sporadically, the primacy of being over whatness but, as Gilson 2002 indicates (163), he has important predecessors:

> Other philosophers had preceded Thomas along this path, and all of them helped him to follow it through to the end, particularly those among them who clearly raised the problem of [being]. Alfarabi, Algazel, Avicenna among the Arabs, Moses Maimonides among the Jews, had already noted the truly exceptional position that [being] occupies in relation to essence ... What seems to have especially intrigued these philosophers is that, however far you push the analysis of essence, [being] must be added to it in some way from outside, as an extrinsic determination conferring on it the act of [being] ... These philosophers started from essence, and using analysis they sought to discover [being] within it, but they

---

[10] Whether, in whatness-frameworks, the whatness of a given thing is an essence shared by other things, or instead the specific thing in its individuality, can be difficult to determine, but is not of importance to *TAPTOE* because in no such framework is being intrinsic either to whatness as universal or to whatness as individual.

The confusion of universal and individual senses of whatness stems most clearly from Aristotle; see Zeller 1897: 329–39, or Bremond 1933: 32–42.

could not find it there. Hence their conclusion: [being] was extraneous to essence as such .... So Alfarabi concludes: "[Being] is not a constitutive factor; it is only an accessory accident."

As this passage makes clear, these predecessors move beyond Aristotle in positing the primacy of whatness not only over attributes, but also over being. Yet if what is called being is extraneous to essence, then essence is extraneous to what is called being. If, however, essence *is*, and is extraneous to what is called being, then what is called being is not being in its ubiquity. Additional steps must be taken.

As indicated above and considered in somewhat more detail below, some of those steps are detectable in various works by Thomas Aquinas although, as shown in *BG* (1.3.2), those works contain no theory of being. Moreover, those works' articulations of being were not widely influential. Indeed, as shown in Gilson 1952 (118), "the genuine meaning of the Thomistic notion of being is, around 1729, completely and absolutely forgotten," thanks chiefly to the dominant influence of Suarez. A revival of so-called existential Thomism develops in the 1930s, and is sufficiently developed by the 1950s that Clarke 1955 includes (61–2) the following announcement:

What is now widely known as the existential interpretation of Thomistic metaphysics has definitely come of age. (By existential I mean that interpretation which sees in the act of existence [*TAPTOE*: being] the source of all perfection and intelligibility, hence the center of gravity of St. Thomas'[s] whole philosophy) ... As speculation and text work proceed hand in hand, each illuminating the other, it is becoming more and more evident that this perspective is by no means some short-lived fad borrowed from the contemporary Existentialist movements and superimposed extrinsically on St. Thomas'[s] own thought, but rather that it is that one luminous center ... in the light of which alone the total body of St. Thomas'[s] texts takes on full intelligibility and coherence.

Fad or not, the revival appears to have been relatively short-lived,[11] and certainly had no influence on the mainstream analytic philosophy that has been dominant since around the time of the revival. Worse yet, as the SSP shows, "the total body of St. Thomas'[s] texts" cannot "[take] on full intelligibility and coherence," not only because the heart of the substance ontology relied on by those texts is unintelligible (see 2.5, above), but also—and more importantly, for this chapter—because although some of those texts recognize the primacy of being, none adequately articulates the ubiquity of being because in them, essence remains somehow distinct from being (see also *BG* 1.3.2.2). The remainder of this section, however, focuses on semantic and ontological problems that would remain even if a variant developed within which essence was fully intrinsic to being.

The semantic and ontological problems endemic to Thomistic being-frameworks are linked to the one identified in a passage from Gilson 1948 considered above. They arise from the at least tacit reliance of Thomistic frameworks on compositional semantics and on ontologies strongly linked to semantically significant grammatical subjects and predicates. The semantic counterparts to

---

[11] It has not utterly disappeared; it remains evident, for example, in Blanchette 2003 and Wippel 2011, but both retain aspects of the Thomistic framework criticized in 2.5, in what follows in this chapter, and in *BG* 1.3.2.

both subjects and predicates are concepts, such that, for example, the sentence "Unicorns are mythological" links the concepts *unicorn* and *mythological*. The semantic status of being, in such frameworks, is problematic because there is no concept that is a counterpart of the word "is" (or "are") in any manner comparable to that in which the concept *unicorn* is the counterpart of the word "unicorn," or the concept *mythological* of the word "mythological." This makes both the semantic and the ontological[12] status of being obscure.

Gilson 2002 (172) addresses this problem by noting initially that "Being is the first of all concepts," because being is co-articulated in every sentence of the form "S is" or "S is p" and, as shown above, any indicative sentence can be rewritten into a sentence with such a form. Being is also, however, "the most universal and abstract [concept], the richest in extension and the poorest in comprehension." It is "richest in extension" because any be-er can be articulated in a sentence whose verb is "is," but "poorest in comprehension" because sentences of the form "S is" can appear to say nothing specific about the be-er that is said by the sentence to be. Because of this poorness in comprehension, Gilson 2002 voices the suspicion that we would need "an intuition of [being]" or an "intellectual intuition of being as being" in order to comprehend it, yet such an intuition would be inarticulable and thus would not make being conceivable. "But," the book continues (174), "reason dislikes what is inconceivable, and because this is true of [being], philosophy does all it can do to avoid it."

---

[12] Because being is not a be-er, the ontological status of being is the status of being in relation to be-ers.

Concerning the articulation of being, then, Thomistic frameworks face first the at least sporadically avoidable problem that, because their sentences at best co-articulate being they tend to place more emphasis on be-ers than on being. This problem is avoided by those who emphasize being, but those who do, even if they also were to recognize the ubiquity of being, would face the insuperable obstacles to clarification of being posed by those frameworks' semantics and ontologies. What is needed, then, if philosophy is to cease to avoid being, is not a new Thomistic theory of being, but instead a different theory of being.[13]

8.3 Central aspects of the SSP's theory of being

8.3.1 The ubiquity, intelligibility, and uniqueness of being

As indicated in various contexts above, the SSP rejects both compositional semantics and any ontology or semantics strongly linked to the structural components of subject-predicate sentences. It links its ontology and semantics instead to sentences with the structure "It's such-and-suching." Because such sentences—technically, sentencings—have no semantically significant subsentential components, their semantics cannot be compositional; it is instead

---

[13] Although Heidegger's works speak at length of being, they do not provide a theory of being, because none relies on an adequately determinable theoretical framework; see *BG*, Chapter 2.

contextual, i.e., one according to which words have determinate meanings only in the contexts of sentences. The semantic contents of sentencings (and sentences) are propositions (technically, propositionings), and these semantic contents relate to the SSP's ontology such that every propositioning is identical to a facting. The absolutely comprehensive facting IT'S BEING (or IT BE BEING) is identical to the true propositioning *It's being* (or *It be being*), which is expressible by the true sentencing "It's being" (or "It be being").

Being as articulated in the sentence "It be being" may appear to be, in Gilson 2002's terms, "universal and abstract," but it is straightforwardly and transparently concretized via that sentence's expansion into the operator "It be being such that," which can govern any and every sentence that expresses a propositioning. An example: "It be being such that it be Alan Whiting such that It be revising It's *TAPTOE*ing"—a sentence true as of the time of its composition. Hence: although being is of problematic intelligibility within the being-frameworks considered and relied on in Gilson's works, because their semantic focus is on concepts and being has, within them, no clear conceptual status, within the framework of the SSP, being is directly articulated by a true sentencing that expresses a true propositioning identical to an actual facting.[14]

---

[14] Gilson 1948 (248) is also instructive:

> it is certain that the concept *being* [*être*] is the only correct conceptual transcription of the meaning connoted by the verb *is*. Thus there is, in the meaning of the verb, something that cannot be conceptualized, but that we nevertheless have the impression of understanding. This amounts to saying that the order of understanding is vaster than is that of the concept or, in other words, that it is possible to know that which it is perhaps impossible to conceive of.

The uniqueness of being mentioned in this subsection's title is clarified by more detailed comparison of being with running (running being simply one of a vast number of possible comparative items). Human be-ers are capable of running or (in slightly different terms) have the capacity to run. The human be-er who runs is activating that capacity—that human be-er be at work running, be engaged in running—whereas the human be-er who sits retains the capacity to run while not activating it, while not engaged in running. In contrast, every human be-er who actually be *cannot avoid* engaging in being, cannot avoid being at work being; any human be-er *not* engaging in being would be a merely *possible* human be-er—like Barack Obama's first grandchild, who does not yet be at the time of *TAPTOE's* completion and may never be—or perhaps a human be-er who, although having been, be no longer.[15] Thus, whereas running is an ontological capacity because human be-ers (along with be-ers of many other kinds) can but need not be engaged in running, being is not a capacity, because human be-ers, along with all other be-ers, have any capacities, activated or not, only if and when they be. This, then, is the most central way that the being of be-ers differs from all of their other engagements: being is the engagement or being-at-work[16] that is not an ontological capacity.

Determining an object of this sort is not a new undertaking. The ways of accomplishing this are well known, [and] *it is no doubt too late to imagine any new ones.* (emphasis added)

Despite this passage's closing phrase, *TAPTOE* provides a new way of articulating being in what is, according to the SSP, its intrinsic intelligibility.

[15] The "perhaps" is included in the sentence to which this note is attached because the question whether, when human be-ers die, they cease to be is one that systematic philosophy must address; see *SB* 4.5.3.4.3.

[16] Classifying being as a mode of being at work or of engagement is meant to increase

The uniqueness of being among the engagements of be-ers is further illuminated by the phenomenon of cryopreservation. Some organisms—including human embryos and adult members of a few species of vertebrates (chiefly amphibians)—can continue to be, and to be the organisms that they are, when they are frozen. When they are frozen, all their metabolic processes cease. Hence, when frozen, they do not activate their capacities for aging or even for living, in anything like the usual sense of living, although they are not dead. They are not dead because they retain the capacity to live; they activate that capacity when they cease to be frozen. Even as frozen, then, they continue to be, to engage in being.[17]

An additional step leads, in a manner different from those introduced above, from the being of be-ers to being itself. No organism has the capacity to bring itself into being, because before the organism is, the organism has no capacities. And yet, the coming into being of the organism reveals that it was possible that the organism come into being. The coming into being of the organism therefore reveals the capacity of being to be manifest, to manifest itself, as that organism. The birth of the organism is being's reconfiguration of itself so as to include that organism; it is the emergence of the organism into and hence within being. For this reason, the gestation of the organism that grows into a salamander is also articulable as being engaging in salamandering: It be being such that it be salamandering.

---

clarity, but it is potentially misleading. Strictly speaking, all of what *TAPTOE* calls beings at work or engagements are modes of being; that it be is requisite to every be-er that be.

[17] Whether adult human beings or indeed all organisms have the capacity of cryopreservation is an empirical question that, at present, remains unanswered.

"Salamandering" is of course a peculiar word, but one whose inclusion in this book should not be surprising, given that one way to be, according to the SSP's ontology, is to be an actual facting identical to a true propositioning expressible by a true sentencing such as, for example, "It's salamandering." A fuller consideration of the "It" in this sentencing further clarifies the involvement of being in salamandering (on this topic, see also *BG* 3.2.1.1).

According to the *Oxford English Dictionary*, the "it" of "It's raining" (and of "It's salamandering") is "the subject of an impersonal verb or impersonal statement, expressing action or a condition of things simply, without reference to any agent." The *OED* includes the following examples: "It has fared badly with the soldiers; How is it in the city? It will soon come to a rupture between them; It is all over with poor Jack; It is very pleasant here." Resituated within the theoretical framework of the SSP, none of these sentences can articulate conditions of *things*, but each can articulate, intelligibly and coherently, configurations of being. That each can is revealed by the fact that each remains intelligible—although, of course, peculiar—if its "it" is replaced with "being": "Being has fared badly with the soldiers; How is being in the city? Being will soon come to a rupture between them; Being is all over with poor Jack; Being is very pleasant here." Given its rejection of the semantics linked to subject-predicate sentences, the SSP cannot of course identify being, in any of these cases, as the *referent* of the "it" that the word "being" replaces. Instead, it takes each "it" to indicate being, a configuration of which is articulated by the words that complete the sentence. Hence, alternative formulations of one of the sentences introduced above include, "Being is no longer configuring itself such that It's

Jacking" and "It's being such that it is no longer the case that It's Jacking."

A further step is taken following introduction of a second instance of the impersonal "it," and one that is of central importance to the SSP. This is the "it" of the theoretical operator, which has the forms "It is the case that" and "It is true that." As explained more fully above (see 3.4–5, 6.3, and 6.3.1.), prefixing the theoretical operator to any indicative (hence, theoretical) sentence can make explicit the semantic status of that sentence. Hence, for example, the semantic status of "It's raining," as asserted, is explicitly articulated in the sentence "It is the case that it's raining."

As *BG* explains, in terms of indicative function, the "it" of any sentencing, such as "It's raining," and the "it" of the theoretical operator are not simply identical. The "it" of "It's raining" indicates a configuration of being at a specific spatio-temporal location. Because, however, the theoretical operator makes explicit the semantic status of *every* theoretical sentence, its scope is absolutely unrestricted: it thus indicates being *as a whole*. The example sentence is thus understood as follows: being *as a whole* is configured such that being here-and-now is configured such that raining is ongoing. Or: It be being as a whole such that It be being here-and-now such that It be raining.

8.3.2 Being and whatness

Indicated above is that a central reason that being-frameworks can be superior to essence- or whatness-frameworks is that whereas even in whatness-frameworks that recognize being, being is extrinsic to essence or whatness, within being-frameworks, essence or whatness can be, for be-ers, intrinsic to their being. To show that and how, according to the SSP, (1) being is prior to the whatness of any be-er and (2) whatness is intrinsic to the being of any be-er, *TAPTOE* introduces two examples, one of a biological be-er's coming- and ceasing-to-be, and one of an artifactual be-er's coming- and ceasing-to-be.

The biological example is a possible case of in-vitro fertilization. Prior to fertilization, there are, of central importance to this example, two be-ers, thus, two be-ers that be, that be engaged in being: these be a sperm cell and an egg cell. If fertilization occurs, egg and sperm will have ceased to be, and a zygote will have come to be. Much about specifically *what* that zygote will be, if it comes to be, is presumably determined by the genetic make-ups of the sperm and egg cells. Yet no matter how great the extent to which *what* the zygote will be, if it comes to be, is determined by the genetics of the sperm and the egg, *whether* the zygote will come to be is *not* determined by those genetic features. *If* the zygote comes to be, it may be *the only zygote* that could have come to be, in this situation, but it will be that zygote only *when it comes to be.* It is, after all, not the case that there is a zygote awaiting entry into being;[18] until the zygote be,

---

[18] Gilson 1948's talk (e.g. 284) of "the essence that receives" the "act of being" results from the chronic failure of Thomistic frameworks to recognize the ubiquity of being; it suggests that the essence, before being, nevertheless somehow *is*, such that it is capable of receiving being.

Blanchette 2003 defends a version of the essence-as-receiver thesis, but does not avoid its problems. At one key juncture, the book argues as follows:

we have in the exercise of judgment a composition of precisely the kind that we claim is the case with *be* as an *act* distinct from its finite essence. It entails a second composition [of act of judging with a specific judgment] that includes a first composition [of subject and predicate in a potential judgment] as one of its members along with there be no zygote. What there be be one cell at work being a sperm cell, and one cell at work being an egg cell; if fertilization occurs, it will be because egg and sperm have jointly reconfigured themselves into constituents of a new be-er, the zygote. But this happens only when the beings-at-work of egg and sperm coalesce into a new being-at-work, that of a zygote. And of course the organism that begins to be as a zygote will, under amenable circumstances, be vigorously at work becoming a blastocyst, then a fetus, then a baby, and so forth.

Considered somewhat differently: sperm and egg are both specific or restricted configurations of being, of being because they be, and specific or restricted because each has specific capacities, and lacks capacities had by other kinds of be-ers; each has the capacity to be for some time, to unite with the other, and, in so uniting, to be reconfigured, or to reconfigure itself, such that some of what had been its constituents become constituents of a zygote. They lack the capacity to be jointly reconfigured, or to jointly reconfigure

---

a proportionally limited act. The composition expressed in the terms of the judgment remains in potency, so to speak, to the proper act of judging, while the same composition limits this act in *receiving* it according to the second composition or that of the judgment as a whole. (358)

Pace this passage's opening sentence, the ontological status of the terms that "receive" the act of judgment, in any case of actual judgment, and of that act, is utterly different from the putative ontological status of the finite essence that is said to receive the act of being, and of that act. In the former case, there be a linguistically competent human be-er to whom the terms usable in any contemplated judgment are already available—they already be, as vocabulary items. So, unless a finite be-er's finite essence and its act of being somehow be before the be-er begins to be—and Blanchette 2003 denies that they precede it in being— Blanchette 2003's composite being is not comparable to its composite judgment. Finally, whereas it is clear that the human being who utters a judgment thereby brings that into being, Blanchette 2003 does not make clear who or what could accomplish the composition of essence and act of being, thereby bringing a be-er into being.

themselves, into anything other than a zygote. If they unite, the zygote will come to be as a specific or restricted configuration of being.

Even if the zygote as a new organism comes to be, it will not, of course, continue forever to be. At some point, it will die—possibly quite abruptly. The physical changes in the organism, when it dies, can appear to be relatively slight, but the ontological change could not be more profound. Following death, many parts of what had been the organism's body may continue to be, and to be at work continuing to be, for some time, but they will no longer be at work as organs, because there will no longer be an organism.

TAPTOE's artifactual example is the following: contemplating what to cook for breakfast, I may narrow my choices to oatmeal and an omelet. If I choose to make the omelet, I have—in one terminology—determined the essence of the be-er that will come to be if I succeed in making it. I can have before me all of the ingredients I will use—eggs and, say, sausage, onion, cheese, and the butter with which I will coat the frying pan—and if I proceed, what omelet will come to be, if an omelet comes to be, is highly determinate. But there is not yet an omelet, and nothing about the possible omelet's essence or whatness determines whether or not it will come to be. What have come to be, already, are the ingredients, with their constituents jointly at work enabling them to continue to be, and I myself, the potential chef. If I opt for the omelet rather than the oatmeal, and if I successfully follow the requisite procedures, the ingredients will begin to work together in such a way that, soon thereafter, an omelet will begin to be. But the beginning to be is the beginning of the omelet—there is no omelet until the omelet be (the omelet I imagine or envisage before I have made it is not a be-er in that it is not engaged in being; my engagement in being includes my imagining or envisaging the omelet, but if I am only imagining or envisaging it, its being is exhausted by its being imagined or envisaged; not so with the omelet that has come to be).

After I have eaten the omelet, of course, the omelet no longer be, but its constituents continue to be, as they—or at least some of them—are reconfigured, temporarily, as constituents of my body.

8.3.3 Neglectfulness of being

This subsection is metasystematic, but is included to further clarify the central importance of being as a topic for systematic philosophy. Its phrase "neglectfulness of being" is a formulation more accurate than the Heideggerian forgetfulness or oblivion of being, mentioned more than once above. The reason for introducing the phrase is suggested by what is said in 8.3.1 about the theoretical operator. Because the theoretical operator indicates and indeed discloses being as a whole, being cannot be wholly absent from *any* theoretical framework. In many—indeed, presumably, in the overwhelming majority—it is tacitly presupposed, and nowhere denied. This is generally wholly non-problematic, although it would be deeply problematic in a systematic philosophy, because any systematic philosophy not including a theory of being would be incomplete. Also deeply problematic, however, are theories that, although (unavoidably) presupposing being, appear to deny being. This is clarified by examples.

8.3.3.1 Recent examples of neglectfulness of being

8.3.3.1.1 Paired philosophical examples: van Inwagen and Lowe 1996

van Inwagen 1996 includes the following (96):

> If the notion of an abstract object makes sense at all, it seems
> evident that if *everything* were an abstract object, if the *only*
> objects were abstract objects, there is an obvious and perfectly
> good sense in which there would be nothing at all, for there would
> be no physical things, no stuffs, no events, no space, no time, no
> Cartesian egos, no God ... When people want to know why there
> is anything at all, they want to know why that bleak state of affairs
> does not obtain.[19]

By "there would be nothing at all," van Inwagen 1996 explicitly means
that there would be no non-abstract objects; there would *be*, in his
scenario, abstract objects, hence *not* the utter absence of being, which
cannot be.[20]

Lowe 1996, a response to van Inwagen 1996, includes (115) the
following:

> Suppose we could show that there *couldn't* be a world containing
> only abstract objects, perhaps by arguing that abstract objects
> necessarily depend for their existence upon concrete objects: what
> would follow? Clearly, it would follow that van Inwagen's 'bleak'

---

[19] Speaking of "states of affairs" as "obtaining" or "not obtaining"—as is common in
mainstream analytic philosophy—is an evasion of being; what could obtaining be other
than being?

[20] Technical clarification of the thesis that absolute non-being cannot be is provided in
8.3.5.

state of affairs couldn't obtain. And yet, in a perfectly clear sense, this wouldn't suffice to show that it was *necessary* for something concrete to exist: for we wouldn't have foreclosed the possibility that *nothing at all*—nothing either concrete or abstract—might have existed. To foreclose that possibility, it seems, we would need also to show that at least some objects, abstract or concrete, exist in every possible world.

For Lowe 1996, the possibility that "*nothing at all*—nothing either concrete or abstract—might have existed" is open if there is a possible world containing no concrete or abstract objects (see 111–12). That possible world would however have to *be* a possible world that would not only itself be but would be distinct from other possible worlds, including the actual world. It would, that is, be situated within being, and would not be—impossibly—the utter absence of being.

8.3.3.1.2 An additional philosophical example: van Inwagen 2008b, 2009

Other works by Peter van Inwagen are among the relatively few by analytic philosophers that recognize that there might be a significant distinction between what *TAPTOE* terms being and be-ers, and hence a need for theories of being. van Inwagen 2008b includes a conversation in which a fictional Alice argues (278) that "*being* is a feature of everything," asking, "who could deny that everything there is *is*?". The conversation leads to "the identification of being with self-identity" (287).[21] The text recognizes as a possible alternative—attributed to

---

[21] A passage from Gilson 1948 quoted above notes that if any sentence of the form "S is" is taken to say that S is itself, it is *not* taken to articulate being.

Sartre, among unnamed others—that being is "an activity that things engage in, the most general activity that they engage in." van Inwagen 2009's treatment of this alternative includes (477) the following (quoted in part in *BG*, 196):

> If there is a most general activity that a human being (or anything else that engages in activities) engages in—presumably it would be something like 'living' or 'getting older'[22]—it is simply wrong to call it 'being'. And it is equally wrong to apply to it any word containing a root related to '*être*' or '*esse*' or '*existere*' or '*to on*' or '*einai*' or '*Sein*' or 'be' or 'am' or 'is'. One cannot, of course, engage in this most general activity (supposing there to be such an activity) unless one *is*, but this obvious truth is simply a consequence of the fact that one can't engage in any activity unless one is: if an activity is being engaged in, there has to be something to engage in it.

As *BG* notes, this passage fails to clarify being because it makes no attempt to explain the "is" of its "unless one is," or the "be" of its "to be something." According to the SSP, if one actually *is*, then one be being, and actually to be something is to be being something.

Perhaps also worth noting is that van Inwagen 2009 attempts to show that being is somehow superfluous or avoidable by introducing a fictional Martian language with the following characteristics:

> There are in Martian no substantives in any way semantically related to '*être*' or '*esse*' or '*existere*' or '*to on*' or '*einai*' or '*Sein*' or

---

[22] The phenomenon of cryopreservation, introduced above, reveals that this is not the case.

'be' or 'am' or 'is'. (In particular, Martian lacks the nouns 'being' and 'existence'... .) There is, moreover, no such verb in Martian as 'to exist' and no adjectives like 'existent' or 'extant'. Finally, the Martians do not even have the phrases 'there is' and 'there are'. (478)

van Inwagen's Martian language does, however, include the following sentences (478–79, emphases added):

Everything *is* not a dragon.

It *is* not the case that everything *is* not (a) God.

I think, therefore not everything *is* not I.

It makes me strangely uneasy to contemplate the fact that it might have *been* the case that everything *was* not always I.

It makes me strangely uneasy to contemplate the fact that everything *is* not (identical with) anything.

It *is* a great mystery why it *is* not the case that everything *is* not (identical with) anything.

As the italicizations clearly show, each of these sentences includes a form of the verb "to be." Being is thus neither superfluous nor avoided in Martian, and it would be open to Martian philosophers to introduce counterparts to "being," "be-er," "It be being," and "It be being such that" into their philosophical languages.

8.3.3.1.3 An example from physics: Krauss 2012

A Universe from Nothing (Krauss 2012) presents itself (xiii) as responding to the question "'Why is there something rather than nothing?'" That, in doing so, it exhibits neglectfulness of being is evident from its assertion (xiv) that "'nothing' is every bit as physical as 'something,' especially if it is to be defined as the 'absence of something.'" Any "nothing" that *is* physical *is not*, obviously, utter non-being. Nevertheless, additional details are worth noting.

According to Krauss 2012 (xvii), "perhaps the most surprising discovery in physics in the past century ... has produced remarkable new support for the idea that our universe arose from precisely nothing." The text later (58) clarifies "precisely nothing" as follows: "By *nothing*, I do not mean nothing, but rather *nothing*—in this case, the nothingness of what we normally call empty space." Yet later (98), this "precisely nothing" is supplemented by several other factors, and becomes "essentially *nothing*": "if inflation indeed is responsible for all the small fluctuations in the density of matter and radiation that would later result in the gravitational collapse of matter into galaxies and stars and planets and people, then it can be truly said that we are all here today because of quantum fluctuations in what is essentially *nothing*." This passage clearly presupposes that matter, radiation, and quantum fluctuations *be*. Moreover, what is first described as empty space is later (104) said to be endowed with energy. As so endowed, it is "Nothing," and (152) it "can effectively create everything we see, along with an unbelievably large and flat universe." And yet:

> it would be disingenuous to suggest that empty space, which drives inflation, is really *nothing*. In this picture one must assume that space exists and can store energy, and one uses the laws of physics like general relativity to calculate the consequences. So if we stopped here, one might be justified in claiming that modern science is a long way from really addressing how to get something

from nothing. This is just the first step, however. As we expand our understanding, we will next see that inflation can represent simply the tip of a cosmic iceberg of nothingness. (152)

So: a universe "created" by empty space endowed with energy is *not*— despite earlier contentions to the contrary—a universe from nothing, and nothingness as a whole is "a cosmic iceberg."

Krauss 2012's cosmic-iceberg sense of nothing/nothingness is (170) "the absence of space and time" but the presence of quantum gravity, and although the text asserts at the outset (xiv) that all of its uses of "nothing" will be "scientific," the following (174) passage indicates that rather than being required by any scientific theory, these uses reflect what "works" for the text's author:

> When I have thus far described how something almost always can come from "nothing," I have focused on either the creation of something from preexisting empty space or the creation of empty space from no space at all. Both initial conditions work for me when I think of the "absence of being" and therefore are possible candidates for nothingness.

The continuation of this passage indicates that neither of these candidates adequately explains the universe as originating from nothing: "I have not addressed directly, however, the issues of what might have existed, if anything, before such creation, what laws governed the creation, or, put more generally, I have not discussed what some may view as the question of First Cause."

The book's suggested answer to this question is the multiverse (175), although the book nowhere asserts that the multiverse is nothing. Instead, it says (177) that "In a multiverse of any of the types that have been discussed, there could be an infinite number of regions, potentially infinitely big or infinitesimally small, in which there is simply 'nothing,' and there could be regions where there is 'something.'" The empty regions would, of course, *be* regions. Be that as it may, the book includes the just-quoted contention about regions in which there is "simply 'nothing'" despite having acknowledged (176) that "we don't currently have a fundamental theory that explains the detailed character of the landscape of a multiverse … (… we generally assume that certain properties, like quantum mechanics, permeate all possibilities …)." In order to permeate all possibilities, the "property" quantum mechanics must of course somehow *be*.

So: Krauss 2012 in fact does not argue that the universe is created from nothing, *even if "create" and "nothing" are understood in the idiosyncratic ways in which that book explains them.* Each of its senses of "nothing" is an absence of be-ers of some kinds or other; each presupposes being.

8.3.4 Being and existing

"Being" and "existing"—or, "to be" and "to exist"—are, in some philosophical frameworks, synonymous. As indicated above, in the SSP's they are not. In the SSP, existence is the mode of being only of factings within the contingently actual dimension of being (this term is fully explained below). Thus: in the SSP's terminology, merely possible worlds and the entities within them are, but do not exist.

One philosopher whose works includes ones that—following works of Quine—equate being with existence is Peter van Inwagen.[23] The difficulties that ensue, particularly in van Inwagen 2008b, are instructive. The following passage (283) provides a fruitful starting point:

> if one says of some woman that she doesn't exist, one *has* to be wrong. If the woman in question is "there" to have something said about her, then she exists.

What, one might wonder, if the woman is "there" in a work of fiction? Of Sherlock Holmes, the text asserts (295) the following:

> There does *exist* such a fictional character as Sherlock Holmes. He is as much a part of the World as is any of the short stories and novels in which he "occurs."

This is problematic at best, because whereas one can buy copies of stories and novels wherein Sherlock Holmes is a character, one cannot acquire the services of Sherlock Holmes; this is a significant *ontological* difference. Moreover, van Inwagen 2008b also asserts (111) the following:

> Words like 'dragon' and 'unicorn' are not names for kinds of non-existent things. Rather, they are not names for anything of any sort, for there are no dragons for them to name.

This introduces an inconsistency: if Sherlock Holmes is "as much a part of the World as is any of the short stories and novels in which

---

[23] On Quine, see *SB* 414 or *BG* 193–94.

he 'occurs,'" then the dragon Smaug is as much a part of the World as is *The Hobbit*. This inconsistency might plausibly result from a failure to adequately revise, given that the passage about Sherlock Holmes appears in the Coda found only in the third edition of van Inwagen's *Metaphysics*, whereas the passage about dragons also appears in the earlier editions. But a comparable inconsistency emerges in the Coda itself. That text denies (296) that "the maps that accompany copies of *The Lord of the Rings* must be maps *of* something," but again, if Sherlock Holmes is a part of what van Inwagen 2008b calls the World because he appears in short stories and novels, then Middle Earth is a part of the World because it appears in novels, and Middle Earth is precisely what the maps accompanying copies of *The Lord of the Rings* are maps of. One might also ask the following: how could the *maps* in *The Lord of the Rings be* maps—rather than mere drawings—if they were not maps *of* anything?

Distinguishing between being and existing facilitates avoidance of problems of the sorts just identified in van Inwagen 2008b. According to the SSP, Sherlock Holmes, Smaug, and Middle Earth do not exist, but each is, within the non-actual world within which it appears.

8.3.5 Dimensions of being

Everywhere, there be being, because all be-ers be, or engage in being. But qualification is necessary, because only actual be-ers be; possible but non-actual be-ers do not. This point may also be put as follows: every actual be-er is *actively* being, is engaged in being. In terms closer to Aristotle's, to be an actual be-er is to be at work being that be-er. For organisms, as indicated above, to die is to cease to be at work being organisms; any organism, having ceased to be at work being an organism, no longer is (or: no longer be).

Because possible but non-actual be-ers are not at work being themselves, their mode of being is derivative (see *SB* 463, 471). There is, then, no be-er at work being Sherlock Holmes. Sherlock Holmes's being is derivative in the first instance from the being-at-work of Arthur Conan Doyle, and in the second instance from the being-at-work of those who read or recall Conan Doyle's novels and stories, and those who present versions of Sherlock Holmes in films, other works of literature, and so forth, and those who assimilate or recall such versions. A volume of Holmes stories on a library shelf is at work preserving those stories, and retains the capacity to present them; that capacity is activated when anyone reads the stories.

These modalities of being—contingently actual being (e.g., of the volume of Holmes stories) and contingently non-actual being (e.g., of Holmes)—require both explanation and supplementation. According to the SSP, there are three distinct modalities of being. Most broadly, there is the absolutely necessary dimension of being and the contingent dimension of being, which can also be termed the dimension of contingent be-ers. The contingent dimension of being includes the dimension of contingently actual be-ers and the dimension of contingently non-actual be-ers. In some other philosophical frameworks, the SSP's dimension of contingently actual be-ers is termed the actual world, and its dimension of contingently non-actual be-ers the realm of merely possible worlds;[24] for convenience, *TAPTOE* occasionally uses this terminology.

According to the SSP, because modalities qualify or determine true propositionings expressible by true sentences or sentencings, and because true propositionings expressible by true sentences or sentencings are identical to actual factings, modalities qualify actual factings. They are, therefore, *being's own* modalities. These modalities of being can be made explicit by means of a number of sentence operators, all of which articulate modalities *of being*. These operators include the following (with examples of arguments included).

1   It is absolutely necessarily the case that it's being.

This is considered below.

2   It is contingently actually the case that there are parents.

There currently are parents, but there is no necessity that there be parents: there were no parents shortly after the Big Bang, and the time may come when there are no longer any parents.

3   It is conditionally necessarily the case that every parent has at least one child.

Because it is only contingently actually the case that there are parents, it is not absolutely necessarily the case that every parent has at least one child. Because however to be a parent is to have at least one child, the modality of the relationship is nevertheless one of necessity.

---

[24] *SB* 5.2.3 clarifies what *TAPTOE* terms the SSP's theory relating the contingently actual dimension of being to the continently non-actual dimension of being, in part by distinguishing it from David Lewis 1986's modal realism, of which it provides a critique.

4 It is contingently non-actually the case that Sherlock Holmes
is a detective (or: It is the case in the contingently non-actual
worlds presented in various stories, novels, and films that
Sherlock Holmes is a detective).

5 It is necessarily not the case that Fred drew a round square.

6 It is necessarily not the case that there is nothing (or: that
nothing is).[25]

Concerning the dimensions of being, the most important of these
sentences are (1) and (6). Both *SB* and *BG* include arguments from
the truth of versions of (6) to the truth of versions of (1). A variant is
the following: By definition, it is possible for any contingent be-er—
and also for being, if all being is contingent being—not to be: for each
contingent be-er, it is possible that it be, and possible that it not be,
so its non-being is possible. If contingent being were exhaustive of
being—if all being were contingent being—then it would be possible
that being not be. But being's not being would be possible only if it
were possible for non-being to be, and that is not possible. Therefore,
being is not exhausted by—is not exhaustively— contingent being, so
must include necessary being as well.

Differently put: it would be *possible* for all being to be contingent being
only if either "It be being such that it be absolutely non-being" or "It be
being such that it be absolute-nothinging" expressed a propositioning,
because if either of these sentencings expressed a propositioning, that

---

[25] Introduction of these operators makes possible expansion of the theory of falsity partially
presented above in 3.5: any sentence expressing a propositioning that is governed by an
operator that mis-situates that propositioning in being is false. Examples: "It is necessarily
the case that *TAPTOE* be," "It is contingently non-actually the case that *TAPTOE* be."

propositioning would be identical to a facting at least in some possible world, and possibly (at some point) in the actual world. But these sentences, like the sentence "Fred drew a round square," do not express propositionings. According to the SSP, they express *pseudo-propositionings*, and pseudo-propositionings are not identical to factings in any world, actual or possible. Such sentences are therefore necessarily false. As indicated in *SB* (239n. 48), the sentence "Fred drew a round square" can be analyzed into the sentences "What Fred drew was round" and "What Fred drew was a square." Each of these sentences expresses a proposition, but the conjunction "What Fred drew was round and was a square," although grammatically correct, does not.

The sentence "It be being such that it be absolutely non-being" is similar, but somewhat more complicated. Its status is clarified by consideration of the more ordinary-sounding "There is nothing," understood as expressing the pseudo-proposition *There is absolute nothingness* or *There is absolute non-being*. What makes these items pseudo-propositions is the fact that sentences of the form "There is such-and-such" express propositions *only if the such-and-such somehow is*. Any such-and-such, however, that in any way is, is not absolute nothingness, not absolute non-being. But if it is not even *possibly* the case that there be nothing, then it is *absolutely necessarily* the case that there be being. Because in addition there are contingent be-ers, hence a contingent dimension of being or dimension of contingent be-ers, being is two-dimensional, including both the contingent dimension of being and the absolutely necessary dimension of being.[26]

---

[26] Because it be possible that the contingent dimension of being not be, the primacy of being is, more specifically, the primacy of the absolutely necessary dimension of being.

The line of thought developed in the preceding paragraph can be put more technically as follows. The theoretical operator formulable as "It be being the case that," which (as explained above in various contexts) implicitly or explicitly governs every indicative sentence, and each of its modal variants ("It be being absolutely necessarily the case that," "It be being contingently actually the case that," and "It be being contingently not actually the case that") situates its arguments *within being*. All propositionings are arguments of such operators, hence so too are the sentences or sentencings expressing them. Pseudo-propositions, however, are not arguments of these operators, but sentences can express pseudo-propositions; those that do are necessarily false. The sentence "It be being such that it be absolute-nothinging" expresses a pseudo-proposition because the "It be being such that" applicable (in one of its forms) to every sentence expressing a propositioning situates that propositioning within being, and absolute-nothinging can in no way be, hence cannot be situated within being.

A final word on this topic may be in order. Such sentences as "Nothing might exist" and "There might someday be nothing" are, of course, grammatically non-problematic. From that it does not follow that they are semantically non-problematic. Again, the same holds for "Fred drew a round square."

8.3.6 Being and God

This section is of course far shorter than the book with which it shares its title, so a reasonable beginning for it is an explanation of the major differences between the two accounts. A thesis central to both accounts is put as follows in *BG* (1): "Any conception of 'God' that is not situated within an explicitly presented or implicitly presupposed theory of being as such and as a whole—and hence, obviously, any such conception presented in conjunction with the rejection of such theories—can only be a conception of something or other, an X, that putatively does or does not 'exist' beyond the world familiar to us and somehow separately from it, but that cannot ultimately be made either intelligible or reasonable." Chapter 1 of *BG* criticizes as inadequate various historical and contemporary approaches to the issue of God that are inadequate because they are *not* situated within theories of being as such and as a whole; *TAPTOE* includes no such critiques. Chapter 2 of *BG* turns to Heidegger, at the heart of whose thought is the question of being, and argues at length that Heidegger utterly fails to respond to that question in a philosophically defensible manner; *TAPTOE* does not repeat that critique. *BG*'s Chapter 3 develops the SSP's theory of absolute being to the point at which coherence and intelligibility are increased by the introduction of the term "God"; *TAPTOE* presents a version of this theory (with minor alterations, and in its different terminology). Chapter 4 of *BG*, finally, criticizes Emmanuel Levinas and Jean-Luc Marion, the most important and influential of those thinkers who attempt—in the language of the central thesis introduced above—to produce conceptions of "God" in conjunction with *rejections* of theories of being. *TAPTOE* does not consider Levinas or Marion.

As indicated in the preceding paragraph, the most important way the SSP's treatment of the issue of God diverges from other treatments of that topic is by situating it within a theory of being as such and as a whole. A second divergence is also worth noting at this point. In contemporary philosophy, the issue "God" is generally treated within what is called philosophy of religion. According to the SSP, this begs various questions and introduces various unnecessary complications. As is clear from (for example) Plato's *Euthyphro* and Aristotle's *Metaphysics*, the issue of God (or gods) is—no matter what else it may be—one that can be treated purely theoretically. That is how the SSP treats it. Consequently, the question addressed in this section is the following: does the inclusion of a facting appropriately designated as God increase the coherence and intelligibility of the SSP?

8.3.6.1 *The relation between the contingent dimension of being and the absolutely necessary dimension of being*

Given the preceding clarifications of the modalities of being and the status of absolute nothingness, the SSP's alternative to the famous but—for reasons just given, incoherent—question "Why is there something rather than nothing?" is easily formulated and explained. The SSP's question is the following: How is the inclusion within being of a contingently actual dimension best explained? There are in principle only three paths for exploration, and two of those paths are merely apparent. The first merely apparent path does not move beyond the contingently actual dimension of being, and thus leads— if it can even be said to lead—only to such responses as "Well, there just *are* contingent be-ers." This "path" that "leads" to such responses is merely apparent because no such response provides an *explanation*. The second merely apparent path would lead to the contingently non-actual dimension of being. That is indeed a distinct dimension of being, but it is one that, as non-actual, has no resources that could explain the inclusion within being of a contingently actual dimension and that, as derivative, cannot in any way be the source of any dimension from which it derives. The exclusion of these two merely apparent paths leaves open only the path to the absolutely necessary dimension of being. Because this is the only path, the questions to be asked are the following: how is that path followed, and where does it lead?

The first step along the path identified in the preceding paragraph consists in determining the relation of the contingent dimension of being to the absolutely necessary dimension of being. According to both *Structure and Being* (454–5, 458) and *Being and God* (234–5), that relation is one of *total dependence*. Why? First, to say that the contingently actual dimension of being is independent of the absolutely necessary dimension of being would be to take the first of the two merely apparent paths rejected in the preceding paragraph. What then if the contingently actual dimension of being were said to be partially dependent on the absolutely necessary dimension of being? Such partial dependence is perhaps posited by some accounts of a *deus absconditus*, according to which God—or, one might say, the absolutely necessary dimension of being—brought the contingently actual dimension of being into being, and then severed relations with it. The problem is that no such account could explain the *continuation in being* of the contingently actual dimension of being; none, that is, could explain why that dimension of being does not cease to be. The thesis that the contingently actual dimension of being is totally dependent on the absolutely necessary dimension of being, however, does explain the continuing being of the contingently actual dimension of being: it is sustained in being by the absolutely necessary dimension of being.

The point made in the preceding paragraph can also be put as follows: being veridically manifests itself, within the theoretical framework of the SSP, such that it includes both an absolutely necessary dimension and a contingently actual dimension, and such that the latter dimension is totally dependent, in being, on the former dimension. Challenges to these theses could be only of two sorts. First, it could in principle be argued that the SSP's theoretical framework would be concretized with greater intelligibility and coherence if one or both of these theses were rejected or altered. Arguments given above in this section at least weigh heavily against any such course of argumentation, and perhaps even show that no such course of argumentation is viable. Second, an alternative theory of being, lacking any version of the theses introduced at the beginning of this paragraph, could develop within an alternative theoretical framework. Were this to happen, that framework could be evaluated at a metasystematic level of the SSP. In the absence of such an alternative theory, objections to the SSP's theory along the lines of "Well, even if it's the best explanation you can come up with, it might not be true" are vacuous. The SSP's explanation *is* true, within its theoretical framework, and *as* true, it articulates factings that are constituents of being.

The next question is, does the total dependence of the contingently actual dimension of being on the absolutely necessary dimension of being make possible the further explication of the absolutely necessary dimension of being? Important to addressing this question is noting the inclusion within the contingently actual dimension of being of human be-ers as be-ers who are, both as thinking and as freely willing, intentionally coextensive with being as such and as a whole, and hence with the absolutely necessary dimension of being. The total dependence of such be-ers on the absolutely necessary dimension of being is however intelligible only if the absolutely necessary dimension of being likewise thinks and freely wills and is thereby intentionally coextensive with being as such and as a whole. Otherwise, what is intelligible to human be-ers would not be intelligible to the absolutely necessary dimension of being. The total dependence of human be-ers, in their being, cannot be explained as a relation to a dimension that is in no way cognizant of them.

The previous paragraph argues that a non-minded absolutely necessary dimension of being is not intelligible as that upon which the contingently actual dimension of being is totally dependent. What, then, of a minded absolutely necessary dimension of being? Such a dimension would not only be cognizant of the contingently actual dimension of being, but would also, as freely willing, be intelligible as that upon which the contingently actual dimension of being would be fully dependent: that there is within being a contingently actual dimension is explained by the free willing, by the absolutely necessary dimension of being, that it be.

In part because the contingently actual dimension of being includes human be-ers who make free decisions, the total dependence of that dimension on the free willing of the absolutely necessary dimension of being cannot be one of being determined in all respects. Instead, according to the SSP, what is freely willed by the absolutely necessary dimension of being is the being, as a whole, of the contingently actual dimension of being. This explains the inclusion within the dimension of being as a whole of the contingently actual dimension of being. Explanations of specific phenomena within the contingently actual dimension of being, on the other hand, are at least in the overwhelming majority of cases explained by other phenomena within that dimension.[27]

At this point, the following question might be raised: even granting that the only way the inclusion within being of a contingently actual dimension can be explained is by its being freely willed by the absolutely necessary dimension of being, might this explanation nonetheless be false? The first thing to be said in response to this possible objection is that *within the theoretical framework of the SSP*, the explanation emerges as true. Because it does, it is the case that this is one of the ways in which being veridically manifests itself within that theoretical framework. The thesis that the inclusion within being of a contingently actual dimension is unintelligible and hence inexplicable cannot be situated within the SSP's theoretical framework given the centrality, to that framework, of the thesis that being is universally intelligible. This of course does not rule out the possibility of theoretical frameworks within which some such thesis could be included, but if some such framework were to be developed and presented, then it could be assessed in comparison with that of the SSP. Only if it proved superior would the SSP give way to it.

8.3.6.2 *God*

Once the absolutely necessary dimension of being has been determined to have freely willed the being of the contingently actual

---

[27] Why the sentence to which this note is appended includes the qualifier "at least in the overwhelming majority of cases" is explained in 8.3.6.4.

dimension of being, and it has been determined, as for example in *TAPTOE* 5.2, that for be-ers within the contingently actual dimension of being it is good to be, it is appropriate to designate the absolutely necessary dimension of being as God.

To further explain this designation of the absolutely necessary dimension of being as God, it is helpful to introduce the principle of rank within being.[28] This principle is the following:

(PRWB) No facting can arise exclusively from or be explained exclusively by any facting of a lower rank within being.[29]

The rank within being of a given facting is determined by the extent of its sphere of influence, the latter understood as including both what the facting can influence, and what can influence the facting. Given this criterion, rocks have a relatively low rank within being, because (for example) they cannot be influenced by threats from animals or from human beings. Because of the ways they interact with other animals and with human beings, animals have considerably higher ranks within being, but because they cannot be influenced by such things as arguments, they rank well below human beings. The sphere of influence of human beings has no limits, in that—given that human beings are intentionally coextensive with being—humans can in principle be influenced by any constituent of being, precisely by thinking about it.

From the PRWB and the total dependence of the contingently

---

[28] The counterpart to this principle in *SB* and *BG* is the principle of ontological rank. *TAPTOE* uses its principle because the absolutely necessary dimension of being has a rank within being, but is not a be-er, and hence has (strictly speaking) no ontological rank. All be-ers, however, do have ontological ranks determined by their spheres of influence, so that term is used, as appropriate, in what follows in the main text.

[29] How the PRWB relates to the theory of evolution is explained in 8.3.6.3.

actual dimension of being on the absolutely necessary dimension of being, it follows that the absolutely necessary dimension of being must be intentionally coextensive with being as such and as a whole, and must be free, because if it were not it would be of a lower rank within being than the human being.

Once the absolutely necessary dimension of being has been determined to be absolutely freely sustaining the being of the contingently actual dimension of being and thus to be appropriately designated as God, two additional lines of inquiry open. Following the first would involve confronting the many problems that arise following the introduction of God into the SSP; prominent among these is the problem of evil.

The second line of inquiry would require the crossing of a methodological watershed. The reason is that additional determination of the absolutely necessary dimension of being, or of God, may become possible through investigation of the contingently actual dimension of being *as wholly dependent on the freedom of God*. The question is, does the course of history provide evidence of God's self-revelation within it such that the interpretive examination of history will make possible further determination of God—possibly as trinity, possibly as having been incarnate? Both *Structure and Being* (459–60) and *Being and God* (3.7.4.1) identify this interpretive examination of history, which could include interpretive examination of such historical texts as the Bible, as a task for the SSP, but neither pursues this task. Nor does *TAPTOE*.

8.3.6.3 *The principle of rank within being and evolution*

Biology, relying on its specific theoretical framework, treats specific empirical questions with specific concepts, assumptions, procedures, etc. Essential is that it establishes that there has been development within the domain of animals and that between the many stages of this development there are similarities and dissimilarities. From this it concludes that there are specific connections between these stages. Finally, it interprets these connections as constituting a history of descent (particularly: human beings are descended from apes). All of this is correct if it is governed by the qualifier "according to the theoretical framework of biology." What that means is, among other things, the following: within that framework, only certain questions are addressed; other questions have no place therein. Among these is the following: How is it possible that such an ascending development can have taken place? How is this ascending development *ultimately* to be explained, particularly given that within it there are be-ers with enormously different ranks within being (and, more specifically, different ontological ranks)?

The first and most central thesis that emerges in the SSP's response to these questions is the following: If a development to higher ontological ranks has taken place, then it was possible for it to have taken place. How is this possibility to be explained? First, this possibility was always a genuine ontological factor included among the entities within the contingently actual dimension of being, where evolution occurs. Already in the earliest and lowest (the purely physical) stages of the cosmos, the possibility for developments to all possible forms and stages, including that for the development of ontologically higher forms, is contained as an immanent factor in the entities found at those stages. If this were not the case, then it would be a miracle that these entities developed as they in fact developed. But how is the immanent ontological status of this possibility of development to be clarified?

The SSP clarifies it as follows: First, comparison of any evolutionarily pre-human organism, with its sphere of influence, with any normal adult human being, with its sphere of influence, indeed reveals that the human's sphere of influence is greater, and thereby that the human being is of a higher ontological rank. But human beings, prior to their emergence in the course of evolution, are not simply absent from the contingently actual dimension of being; they are instead *ontologically* included within this dimension of being *as possibilities*, in that *if and when* the requisite complex configuration of non-human factings emerges, that configuration will be a human being. The emergence of human beings in the course of evolution is thus nothing like a teleportation from the contingently non-actual dimension of being (or: from some merely possible world) into the contingently actual dimension of being. Instead, prior to the emergence of human be-ers in the course of evolution, there be non-human be-ers that have the capacity, in conjunction, to reconfigure themselves such that they cease to be when be-ers of higher ontological ranks, and eventually human be-ers, come to be. The span of time, whatever its extent, that precedes the emergence of human beings within the contingently actual dimension of being is thus a *gestation period* for human beings. The same holds for organisms of all other kinds.

8.3.6.4 *The SSP and Christianity*

According to *Structure and Being* (332), "within the philosophical perspective developed here, Christianity is the incomparably superior religion." The SSP includes this thesis because Christianity satisfies an explicitly identified criterion (443): "only Christianity has developed a *genuine* theology: one that satisfies the highest demands and challenges of theoreticity." The Christian religion thus provides the theoretician working within the framework of the SSRPP with a potentially valuable starting point in that Christian theology provides the theoretician with data potentially incorporable into its theory of God. That no other religion provides such data is an empirical thesis. If it were shown to be false, or if it were to become false in the future— if a genuinely theoretical theology linked to any other religion were developed, identified, or discovered—then that theology, too, would provide data potentially incorporable into the SSP.

In part because Christian theology provides data for potential incorporation into the SSP, *Being and God* envisages, as the first central question to be addressed as the SSP seeks to further develop its theory of God by examining the history of the contingently actual dimension of being, the question of the degree to which God as articulated by that theory can be identified as the adequately articulated biblical-Christian God (see 252–3). It also, however, explicitly recognizes (271–2) the possibility that that degree would be insignificant. In addition, theoreticians working to further develop the SSP's theory of God could focus on religions other than Christianity. Whether historical investigation will make possible further determination of God as articulated by the SSP and, if it does, how closely

God, as further determined within the SSP, will resemble the God of any religion, are at this point open questions.

A final remark is in order. It concerns the relation between engaging in philosophy and being of religious faith. As *Being and God* explains in greater detail (281–2), the philosopher who *as a philosopher* engages in theorization about God *may or may not* also be of religious faith, Christian or otherwise, and the Christian or person of other religious faith may or may not engage in philosophy. The philosopher who is not of religious faith may or may not be led by theoretical engagement with the issue of God to become of religious faith, Christian or otherwise, and the philosopher who is a Christian or of other religious faith may or may not be led by their theoretical engagement to alter or abandon that faith.

WORKS CITED

Aristotle. (2002), *Metaphysics*. Translated and edited by Joe Sachs. Second edition. Cambridge, MA: Green Lion Press.

—(1994), *Posterior Analytics*. Translated and with a Commentary by Jonathan Barnes. Oxford: Oxford University Press.

Armstrong, D. M. (1984), 'Consciousness and causality'. In D. M. Armstrong and N. Malcolm, *Consciousness and Causality*, Oxford: Blackwell, 103–91.

Blanchette, O. (2003), *Philosophy of Being. A Reconstructive Essay in Metaphysics*. Washington, DC: Catholic University of America Press.

Boland, L. A. 1982. *The Foundations of Economic Method*. London: George Allen & Unwin.

Bremond, A. (1933/1987), *Le Dilemme Aristotélicien*. Paris: G. Beauchesne (rep. edn). New York: Garland.

Clarke, W. N. (1955), 'What is really real?' In J. A. Williams (ed.), *Progress in Philosophy. Philosophical Studies in Honor of Rev. Doctor Charles A. Hart*. Milwaukee: Bruce Publishing Co., 61–90.

Cory, H. E. (1947), *The Significance of Beauty in Nature and Art*. Milwaukee: Bruce Publishing Co..

Diels, H. (1996), *Die Fragmente der Vorsokratiker. Griechisch und Deutsch*, (12th unchanged edn), Walther Kranz (ed.). Vol. 1. Dublin and Zürich: Weidmann.

Euclid. (2002), *Euclid's Elements*. Translated by T. L. Heath, edited by Dana Desnmore. Cambridge, MA: Green Lion Press.

Field, H. (1972), 'Tarski's theory of truth'. *The Journal of Philosophy* 69: 347–75.

Fromkin, V., Rodman, R., and Hyams, N. (2011), *An Introduction to Language* (9th edn). Boston: Wadsworth.

Frye, N. (1964/2000), 'Convocation address, Franklin and Marshall'. In G. S. French., N. Frye, and J. O'Grady (eds) (2000), *Northrop Frye's Writings on Education*. Toronto: University of Toronto Press.

Gettier, E. (1963), 'Is justified true belief knowledge?' *Analysis* 23: 121–3.

Gilson, É. (1948), *L'Être et L'Essence*. Paris: Librairie Philosophique J. Vrin.

—(1952), *Being and Some Philosophers* (2nd edn). Toronto: Pontifical Institute of Mediaeval Studies.

—(2002), *Thomism. The Philosophy of Thomas Aquinas. A Translation of* Le Thomisme (6th and final edn). Translated by L. K. Shook and A. Maurer. Toronto, ON: Pontifical Institute of Mediaeval Studies.

Grayling, A. C. (ed.) (1999), *Philosophy. A Guide Through the Subject*. Oxford: Oxford University Press.

Harper, D. A. (1996), *Entrepreneurship and the Market Process. An enquiry into the growth of knowledge*. London and New York: Routledge.

Hawking, S. (2001), *The Universe in a Nutshell*. New York: Bantam.

Hodgson, D. (2005), 'A plain person's free will'. *Journal of Consciousness Studies* 12:1, 1–19.

t' Hooft, G., Susskind, L., Witten, E., Fukugita, M., Randall, L., Smolin, L., Stachel, J., Rovelli, C., Ellis, G., Weinberg, S., and Penrose, R. (2005), 'A theory of everything?' *Nature*, Vol. 433, No. 7023, January 20: 257–9.

Horwich, P. (2001), 'A defense of minimalism'. In M. P. Lynch (2001), *The Nature of Truth. Classic and Contemporary Perspectives* : 559–77.

van Inwagen, P. (1996), 'Why is there anything at all?' *Proceedings of the Aristotelian Society. Supplementary Volumes*. Volume 70: 95–110.

—(2003), 'Existence, Ontological Commitment and Fictional Entities'. In M. J. Loux and D. W. Zimmerman (eds). *The Oxford Handbook of Metaphysics*. Oxford: Oxford University Press, 131–57.

—(2008a), 'How to think about the problem of free will.' *Ethics* 12: 327–41.

—(2008b), *Metaphysics* (3rd edn). Boulder, CO: Westview Press.

—(2009), 'Being, existence, and ontological commitment'. In D. Chalmers, D. Manley, and R. Wasserman (eds), *Metametaphysics. New Essays on the Foundations of Ontology*. Oxford: Clarendon Press.

Kane, R. (2001), 'Introduction: The Contours of Contemporary Free Will Debates'. In R. Kane (ed.) *The Oxford Handbook of Free Will*. 2nd edn. Malden, MA: Blackwell.

—(2005), *A Contemporary Introduction to Free Will*. Oxford and New York: Oxford University Press.

Kant, I. (1998), *Critique of Pure Reason*. Translated by Paul Guyer and Allen Wood. Cambridge and New York: Cambridge University Press. Following long-standing practice, "A" indicates the first (1781) edition, "B" the second (1787).

—(2000), *Critique of the Power of Judgment*. Translated by P. Guyer and E. Matthews. Cambridge and New York: Cambridge University Press.

Kovach, F. J. (1974), *Philosophy of Beauty*. Norman, OK: University of Oklahoma Press.

Krauss, L. (2012), *A Universe from Nothing. Why Is There Something Rather Than Nothing*. New York: Free Press.

Ladyman, J. and Ross, D. (2009), *Everything Must Go: Metaphysics Naturalized*. New York: Oxford University Press.

Libet, B., Freeman, A., and Sutherland, K. (eds) (1999), *The Volitional Brain*. Thorverton: Imprint Academic.

Libet, B., Gleason, C., Wright, E., and Pearl, D. (1983), 'Time of conscious intention to act in relation to onset of cerebral activities (readiness potential): the unconscious initiation of a freely voluntary act'. *Brain* 106, 632–42.

Lowe, E. J. (1996), 'Why is there anything at all?' *Proceedings of the Aristotelian Society. Supplementary Volumes.* Volume 70: 111–20.

Lynch, M. P. (2001), *The Nature of Truth. Classic and Contemporary Perspectives.* Cambridge, MA: MIT Press.

Mackie, J. L. (1977/1990), *Ethics. Inventing Right and Wrong.* Harmondsworth: Penguin.

Matson, W. I. and Fogelin, R. J. (1988), *A New History of Philosophy.* San Diego: Harcourt, Brace, Jovanovich.

McGinn, C. (2003), 'Isn't it the truth?' *The New York Review of Books*, April 10, 70–3.

—(2003), *Logical Properties. Identity, Existence, Predication, Necessity, Truth.* Oxford: Oxford University Press.

Nagel, T. (1987), *What Does It All Mean? A Very Short Introduction to Philosophy.* Oxford and New York: Oxford University Press.

Neurath, O. (1921), Anti-Spengler. In Otto Neurath, *Empiricism and Sociology.* Edited by M. Neurath and Robert S. Cohen. Boston: Reidel, 1973. 158–213.

Oxford English Dictionary (1989), *OED*, (3rd edn). Oxford: Clarendon Press.

Puntel, L. B. (2006), *Struktur und Sein. Eine Theorierahment für eine systematische Philosophie.* Tübingen: Mohr Siebeck.

—(2008), *Structure and Being. A Theoretical Framework for a Systematic Philosophy.* Translated by and in collaboration with A. White. University Park, PA: Penn State University Press.

—(2010), *Sein und Gott. Ein systematischer Ansatz in Auseinandersetzung mit M. Heidegger, É. Lévinas und J.-L. Marion.* Tübingen: Mohr Siebeck.

—(2011), *Being and God. A Systematic Approach in Confrontation with Martin Heidegger, Emmanuel Levinas, and Jean-Luc Marion.* Translated by and in collaboration with A. White.

—(2012), *Estructura y Ser. Un Marco Teórico para una Filosofía Sistematica.* Buenos Aires: Prometeo Libros.

Putnam, H. (1967), 'Time and physical geometry'. *The Journal of Philosophy* 64:8, 240–7.

—(1994), 'The Dewey lectures 1994: sense, nonsense, and the senses: an inquiry into the powers of the human mind'. *The Journal of Philosophy* 91: 445–518.

Quine, W. Van Orman (1960), *Word and Object.* Cambridge, MA: MIT Press.

—(1970), *Philosophy of Logic.* Englewood Cliffs, NJ: Prentice-Hall.

—(1992), *Pursuit of Truth* (rev. edn). Cambridge: Harvard University Press.

Roche, C., Month, M., Lindecker, G., and Gelès, C. (1999), *Managing Science: Management for R&D Laboratories*. New York: Wiley-VCH.

Russo, L. (2004) *The Forgotten Revolution. How Science Was Born in 300 bc and Why It Had to Be Reborn*. Berlin: Springer.

Schwartz, S. P. (2012), *A Brief History of Analytic Philosophy. From Russell to Rawls*. Chichester, Malden, MA and Oxford: Wiley-Blackwell.

Smart, J. J. C. (2005), 'Comments on Hodgson'. *Journal of Consciousness Studies* 12:1, 58–64.

Soames, S. (2003), *Philosophical Analysis in the Twentieth Century, vol. 2: The Age of Meaning*. Princeton: Princeton University Press.

Soon, C. S., Brass, M., Heinze, H.-J., and Haynes, J.-D. (2008), 'Unconscious determinants of free decisions in the human brain'. *Nature Neuroscience* 11: 543–5.

Strawson, G. (2003), 'What is the relation between an experience, the subject of the experience, and the content of the experience?' *Philosophical Issues* 13, 279–315.

—(2006), 'Realistic monism: why physicalism entails panpsychism'. *Journal of Consciousness Studies* 10–11: 3–31.

—(2008), 'The impossibility of ultimate moral responsibility'. In G. Strawson, *Real Materialism and Other Essays*. Oxford: Oxford University Press, 319–31.

Strawson, P. F. (2004), 'Truth'. In *Logico-Linguistic Papers*. Revised edn. Burlington, VT: Ashgate, 147–64.

Tarski, A. (1933/1956), 'The concept of truth in formalized languages'. In Tarski, *Logic, Semantics, Metamathematics. Papers from 1923 to 1938*. Oxford: Clarendon, 152–278.

—(1944), 'The semantic concept of truth and the foundations of semantics'. *Philosophy and Phenomenological Research* 4: 341–76.

Tatarkiewicz, W. (1980), *A History of Six Ideas. An Essay in Aesthetics*. The Hague and Boston: Springer.

—(1995/2005), *History of Aesthetics* (3 vols). London and New York: Continuum International Publishing Group.

Taylor, R. (1961/1992), *Metaphysics*. East Rutherford, NJ: Prentice-Hall.

Thornton, B. S. (1999), *Plagues of the Mind. The New Epidemic of False Knowledge*. Wilmington, DE: ISI Books.

Verdenius, W. J. (1962), Science grecque et science moderne. *Revue Philosophique de la France et de l'Étranger*. 82: 319–36.

Wegner, D. M. *The Illusion of Conscious Will*. Cambridge, MA: MIT Press.

Weinberg, S. (1992), *Dreams of a Final Theory*. New York: Pantheon Books.

Weiss, M. and Hoover, K. H. (1964), *Scientific Foundations of Education*. Dubuque, IA: William C. Brown Co.

Wippel, J. F. (2011), 'Thomas Aquinas on the ultimate why question: why is there anything at all rather than nothing whatsoever?' In J. F. Wippel (ed.), *The Ultimate Why Question. What Is There Anything at All Rather than Nothing Whatsoever?* Washington, DC: The Catholic University of America Press.

Wittgenstein, L. (2001), *Philosophical Investigations. The German Text, with a Revised English Translation.* Translated by G. E. M. Anscombe. Oxford: Blackwell.

Wolpert, L. (1993/1998), *The Unnatural Nature of Science.* Cambridge, MA: Harvard University Press.

Zeller, E. (1897), *Aristotle and the Earlier Peripatetics. Being a Translation from Zeller's* Philosophy of the Greeks. Translated by B. F. C. Costelloe and J. H. Muirhead. Vol. 1. London, New York and Bombay: Longmans, Green, and Co.

INDEX

Boldface entries are to subsections not included in the Table of Contents.